THE

CASTAWAY

SURVIVAL
GUIDE

THE

CASTAWAY

SURVIVAL
GUIDE

ROBIN EGGAR

First published in Great Britain in 2007 by
Virgin Books Ltd
Thames Wharf Studios
Rainville Road
London
W6 9HA

A catalogue record for this book is available from the British Library.

ISBN 978-1-905264-00-1

The paper used in this book is a natural, recyclable product made from wood grown
in sustainable forests. The manufacturing process conforms to the regulations of the
country of origin.

Printed and bound in the United Kingdom

Designed and typeset by Virgin Books Ltd

Contents

Introduction

Imagine you find yourself castaway in a strange environment with precious little kit. What can you expect? What do you do first?

It's not just the immediate practical problems of surviving and wondering how you will look with filthy hair or a very shaggy beard. You must also learn how to overcome psychological challenges you will never have faced before. Can you cope with being a lone castaway, or part of a castaway group, which can be even worse? Famous castaway tales provide encouragement, but also serve as warnings about what can go horribly wrong.

Once you get used to and start to master your environment, the emphasis changes from what is necessary for basic survival to what can make your life more pleasant, even fun. Why screw up your eyes when you can make sunglasses out of bark? Why force down another worm when the finest organic ingredients are just waiting to be made into a castaway feast?

As the book progresses, you will build up expertise and confidence. It's all here – from comfortable beds to hunting, fishing and cooking techniques, even home-brewed booze – all from the most basic materials and tools.

However life's full of surprises and shit happens ... generally when you least expect it. Advice on dealing with diseases, insects, natural disasters and hungry predators accompanies each chapter, and should the castaway idyll go belly up, you'll need the extreme survival techniques and escape strategies described at the end of the book.

In essence it boils down to the old Boy Scout motto – "Be prepared".

Enjoy ... grubs, snails and all.

DON'T PANIC!

CASTAWAY

'It is not easy for any one, who has not been in the like
condition, to describe or conceive the consternation of men
in such circumstances; we knew nothing where we were, or
upon what land it was we were driven ...'

Daniel Defoe, *Robinson Crusoe*

Where are you?

Wow! You're sitting on a stunning white-sand beach in the baking sun. The
sea is so blue it melds seamlessly into the sky. There is no vulgar scramble
for the sun loungers because there are no sun loungers. There is also no
cute shack serving rum punches in hacked-out coconuts because there
don't appear to be any coconuts.

This is a worry because there is almost no better friend to a castaway. But,
coconuts or not, there are a lot of trees and greenery around. That means
there's water. Good. Without water you're in serious trouble.

You're thinking. Excellent. Keep your head clear. Deep breaths in through
the nose, hold it, let the air trickle out through your mouth. Get the
heartbeat down. If your heart's pounding faster than a drum'n'bass special
you're close to panic. Panic can kill. It doesn't matter if you've been caught
in an avalanche, involved in a car smash or woken up to find yourself in a
28 Days Later post-Armageddon scenario, you have to think to survive.

If you give up you will die, so think and act positive.

Right now, why you're here is not important. That can come later. Accept
the fact that you find yourself in an unexpected situation, an alien and
potentially hostile environment, and that to survive you will have to learn
to think differently. And you will have to learn fast.

The first rule is stay where you are or as close as possible to where you
first found yourself in trouble. Rescuers start looking at the last known
point of contact and then fan out from there. Think smart. If your car has

broken down on a forest road don't wander off into the woods in search of the gingerbread house.

Provided nobody is injured, the immediate threats to your survival are environmental. If it is cold, get out of the wind any way you can. Wind chill doubles the chance of exposure, frostbite or hypothermia. Find natural shelter or, if necessary, create it by piling up rocks, wood, backpacks – any bulky objects you have to hand to fashion a makeshift windbreak.

On the beach it's hot and getting hotter. First thing to do is get off the sand and under some shade. Avoid the temptation to top up your tan or flash your biceps. The sun is your enemy. If you can't find shade, make it. The debilitating effects of sunburn or heatstroke may not be that easy to treat in your new circumstances. Keep your clothes on also, maximising the cooling effect of your sweat. Move slowly. Conserving energy helps retain fluid for as long as possible. Our body constantly processes and recycles water – we lose an average of 2-3 litres (3.5–5 pints) each day. The more we exert ourselves, the hotter the temperature, the more water we lose.

In the shade, take a while to gather your senses. Prioritise. To survive indefinitely you need four things: shelter, food, water and fire. Your circumstances and environment will determine your immediate needs. What do you have to do to survive tonight?

⚭ The rule of threes
To cope with extreme conditions remember this mantra. A person can survive for:
- three minutes without air,
- three hours without shelter,
- three days without water,
- three weeks without food.

It is not an absolute, but, assuming you are still breathing, it is worth following. Decide on your most important basic need and start on it immediately.

In most survival situations a shelter should be built first. If you're stuck up a mountain, rain, snow and high winds or a combination of all three can quickly lead to exposure, so your first priority is to seek shelter. When you're exhausted, rest and recuperation are paramount. Shelter protects you from potentially disastrous weather, helps prevent hypothermia and allows sleep. It will also boost morale by providing a base or home.

Your most basic level of shelter is clothing – don't underestimate the protection secured by pulling on another layer of clothes, draping yourself in a blanket or even covering yourself in a pile of leaves. After this comes minimal short-term protection – something to get you through the first night or two. For longer-term shelter, it will take time to find the right location and create the most effective structure.

✍ Protection from the elements

Finding an immediate shelter
Do you know the time, and when the sun sets? The closer you are to the equator, the shorter the twilight. You need to have established your chosen campsite a good hour before darkness falls. Fluffing up pillows can be done in the dark; finding them can't.

A shelter should be a relatively comfortable place to sleep. When looking for the right location, consider the following. Avoid immovable rocks, animal nests and other obstacles and hazards. Dry watercourses may be flat, sandy and comfortable to sleep on, but they will flood in a storm. Sunlight will provide warmth (not always welcome), and help one to wake up in the morning. However, sunny, open areas are vulnerable to wind.

Four elements to remember when building your shelter

SHINGLES: Keep you dry and protect you from the heat of the sun.

FIRE: Keeps you warm.

INSULATION: Traps available heat inside. In the long run insulation conserves energy. Spending hours gathering firewood to keep warm is counterproductive.

AIRPROOFING: Stops cold drafts of air.

Staying dry is most important. It's easier to get warm if you're not soaked through. The trick is to cover your shelter with shingling.

Your home has shingles. Whatever your roof is made of – tiles, asphalt carpet, corrugated iron slabs – its function is to drain off rain or snow and keep you nice and dry. Out in the wild there is plenty of shingling available. It doesn't come with a white van, an infinite capacity for tea and excuses and a larger-than-expected bill. In the bush, shingling can be found in tree bark, logs, overhead branches, leaves, clods of earth, boulders and rock overhangs – or a combination of all of them.

First night shelter

Start by looking for any abandoned buildings or dry caves within five minutes of the beach. Walls are always better than no walls. With caves, check for animal or other occupants and give them an escape route. Establish the high tide line on the beach. Otherwise make do with what is immediately available and search for the best natural shelter from the elements. Find a patch of ground, free from risk of flooding, rock falls, falling branches or avalanches. Improve on it by building a low wall of stones caulked with moss or mud. Keep it simple to save energy.

CASTAWAY

Basic frame shelter

Life does get a whole lot simpler if you are in possession of a tarpaulin, sheets of plastic or even a lightweight rain poncho. *In extremis* you can just wrap yourself up in it, sit up against a tree and wait for morning.

To make a basic frame tent remove stones and twigs and stamp the ground down. This will make for a much better night's sleep. Plan the entrance on the side facing away from the wind. Your goal is to build a structure in the classic triangular tent shape, with a long pole supported by two sticks at either end. Ideally the ridgepole should be 3.5 metres (about 12 feet) long. The two sticks holding it up should be jammed into the ground around 2 metres (6 to 7 feet) apart. A few more sticks for the frame, and then you cover it with the sheeting. If you have plenty of material you could fit a second shelter a few centimetres above the first, cutting back the chances of nasty leaks during the night. Where possible, fold the sheet under your body as well. If you don't have enough manmade material, cut boughs or fronds off trees.

With no sheeting, lash living saplings together and then weave in smaller branches and cover with turf – a living tepee (or tipi). You can build a simple lean-to by tying a stick between two trees, then leaning more sticks on it to form a triangular structure. Insulate further by covering it with leafy branches and leaves (and, if appropriate, snow). Putting earth, sand or mud around the base of the structure will give it more strength. If there is time, surround the structure with a shallow ditch to avoid the risk of waking up soaked through.

Use the natural features of the environment and then add to them. A thick canopy of leafy branches acts as a first layer of protection. Look for a fallen tree with space to crawl underneath. Then lean slabs of bark or branches against the side to increase the dry space. If the bark slabs go over the top of the log any falling water will follow the straight line down rather than curve around the log and drip on your nose all night. A fallen tree with exposed roots is a natural windbreak – just fill in the gaps between the

roots. In dire straits hollow out one side of a fallen tree trunk – the side that faces away from the sea unless the wind is blowing off the land. You need a windbreak, not a wind tunnel.

If there are boulders around, they can provide a natural wall or a partial roof that you can enhance with bark slabs and logs. But moisture will follow the contours of the rock, so, to avoid a soggy bum, study the moss. The long narrow lines of moss on the underside of your chosen home are baby canals. You will have to find ways of diverting the flow.

If all else fails, look for a natural hollow in the ground. If it's too shallow you can dig it out, then lay branches across the hole. To gain elevation place a higher log on top of the branches to give yourself a natural gable and roof pitch which water can drain off, then cover with shorter sticks, turf, bark leaves or grass. If it is on a slope, make sure you deflect water before it turns your shelter into a mud bath.

A basic shelter

Use what's around you. In a forest with a deep layer of leaves, use them to build a 'debris hut'. The inside is an organic sleeping bag. Start with a classic tent shape – a skeleton of wood boughs resting on the diagonal against a horizontal ridgepole. Then heap on the leaves at least 60cm (2 feet) deep. Also, line the inside with soft and dry grass, leaves and moss for extra insulation. In a debris hut you don't need fire, because your body heat will generate enough warmth. Who needs a sleeping bag?

Whatever shelter you find, try to get your body off the earth. In tropical jungle, a myriad biting and crawling things lurk on the ground. If nothing else, clear the sleeping area of any protruding rocks and lay out a mattress of leaves, palm fronds, cardboard packaging – anything dry. This is more than a comfy bed: it's an insulating pad between your body and the earth. Dampness and cold coming up through the ground can chill you to the bone wherever you are. The rule is that you should have twice as much insulation below you as above you. It won't be the Ritz, but you won't have to tip the staff for opening the door.

Preparing a fire

If you can start a fire easily without wasting vital resources of fuel or matches, then do so, even if gaining warmth, for now, does not seem important. Do not assume that hot days ensure balmy evenings. During the first Gulf War the elite SAS troop Bravo Two Zero were undone by the freezing desert nights. Fire also protects from potential predators and can send signals if immediate rescue is a possibility. You may well need to boil water or cook food.

Perhaps just as important is the civilising instincts it arouses inside us. Sitting around a fire makes you feel as if there is hope. It relaxes, calms, provides a warm inner glow – and it's a great medium for encouraging group communication.

For now you should concern yourself with only the basics of fire making. Clear a sheltered spot. If there is no such thing available, then dig a trench in the ground and light the fire there. If you are the lucky occupant of a cave, plan the fire at the back, since this actually helps the smoke find its way out of the entrance.

Do not forget the Fire Pyramid. The four sides stand for air, heat, fuel and uninhibited chain reactions. Take one away and the pyramid collapses and the fire goes out. Easiest for inexperienced firelighters to forget is air – or

ventilation. The more oxygen, the brighter the fire burns. Reduce the air coming in and the less it burns.

Assemble everything you need before you start – tinder, kindling and fuel. Think how much fuel you will need, then double it. Keep it in your shelter and to hand, so that you don't need to venture out once you are warm.

Tinder
This is anything that can be ignited by an incendiary spark. It needs to be dry – as in 'tinder-dry'. Take your pick from: paper, wood shavings, dry bark or grass, cotton fluff from your coat or fibrous strips from the inner bark of a dead tree. If stuck, use tampons or your own hair (just make sure you cut it off first). Less obvious but equally effective are dried fungi crumbled into a powder, the fine dust produced by wood-burrowing insects (look inside a dead log) or the inside of birds' nests.

Kindling
Use bark or small dry twigs from resinous and soft wood (pine, chestnut and willow). Again, this must be completely dry, so don't collect it from the ground unless that is bone-dry too. If the outside of the wood is damp to the touch, shave off the bark and wood layers with a knife or sharpened rock until you reach a layer of dry wood. Pine, fir and spruce needles and cones are all very effective, though putting on too many needles can douse a fledgling flame.

If dry kindling is scarce you can make 'feather sticks'. Find a dead tree that is still standing vertical and that you cannot encircle with both hands (otherwise the wood may be wet to the core). Split the wood into thumb-thick pieces that stretch from elbow to fingertip. Then cut down on one side of the wood only with the curved portion of a sharp blade to make as many shavings as possible (see the diagram on page 18). Each shaving should run up to three-quarters of the stick and should have more than one complete curl. The more curls you can get on one piece of wood the better. The curl ignites quickly and if enough heat is generated the rest of the wood should catch before the flame goes out.

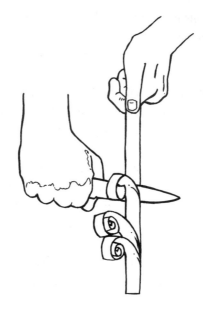

A Feather Stick

Fuel

Everything else that burns. Peat and animal dung are the last resorts.
When it is wet, look for dry dead wood caught in the cracks or between the
branches of live trees.

Prepare a fire shape that looks like a tepee with kindling twigs crisscrossed
and freestanding above a tinder bed. Beware: if the tinder is too densely
packed there will not be enough oxygen to reach the flame. In very windy
conditions build a lean-to fire. Find a large log, put your face into the wind
and build the nest of tinder in the lee of the log. Then lay the kindling
across the nest with the tops resting on the log – just like a lean-to shelter.

Lighting a fire with one match

Matches are precious. (No matter how successful a castaway you become
it will be many years before you start making matches.) They are also
the easiest way to start a fire. Any match will do, though a book of paper
matches don't strike so well, burn out quickly and dissolve if they get wet.

Waterproof matches are best and the non-safety type are easier to strike. For added rainproofing, dip the heads in candle wax. The experts split matches (even paper ones) in two. Double your resources.

When striking a match, shield the flame with your cupped hand, then hold the tip downward and let the flame burn up towards your fingers. This helps the flame grow large enough to light something else before it goes out.

Once the tinder has caught, the oxygen will generate enough heat for the kindling to catch. With the fuel, start with smaller branches and logs ranging from thumb to arm width. As the heat of the fire increases you can drag on bigger and bigger logs, mixing up green and dead wood. Soft woods such as pine burn very quickly, can crackle, bang and shoot off sparks. Hard woods – hickory, beech, oak – last much longer and give off more heat. Lay them at a slight angle to each other. The spread of a fire is confined to the area where the spacing between logs is less than 10cm (4 inches). You can also lay long logs crisscrossed in a star shape. The fire burns only where the sticks cross. The bigger that area, the bigger the fire. As the logs burn through simply push them into the middle to catch.

Don't see it as an insult to your pyromaniac self if the wood is damp and the fire smokes heavily – it is a better signal and helps keep insects away. Look for the positives. The stones you put around the fire to shelter it will turn out to be great bed warmers.

Once you are warm and at least minimally sheltered, there is time to think.

〰 What have you got that will help you survive?

Do an inventory of everything you have with you – but you must pool everything. If you are alone it is simple: you have only yourself to rely upon; screw up, and *you* pay the consequences. Being part of a group will lead to different problems, but right now that's not important.

Don't throw anything away. It may come in useful in ways you never imagined possible. Every single thing you possess has a value – even a paper bag with a hole in it. A successful survivor is a scavenger, a beachcomber and a lateral thinker.

You are probably much better equipped than you thought.

21 things you might have, and some of their uses

COINS: Bigger coins can be sharpened for cutting; can be used to weight fishing lines and nets.

PENKNIFE: Keep it close and the blade sharp.

TORCH: Keep for nighttime emergencies and exploring cave systems. Don't waste the batteries. Reverse batteries to prevent using them unnecessarily.

PLASTIC BAGS: Invaluable. Can be used for capturing water off trees and for rainproofing shelters. If you don't have any, take a look along the beach. The chances are high that there will be something plastic in the sand.

SMALL BOTTLE OF WATER: Don't break it – it's the best way of transporting water you will have.

CREDIT CARDS: Hard plastic edges can be used to descale and gut fish.

MOBILE PHONE: Assuming that there is no signal, the innards can be scavenged. Also, camera lenses can be used to focus sunlight for fire lighting.

KEYS: Anything metal can be sharpened and used as a tool, or polished and used as a fishing lure.

LIPSTICK: Can be used to prevent chapped lips or as a sunburn preventative, or even as a soothing treatment for minor scratches and abrasions. It can also be used as a direction marker or for writing messages.

KEY RINGS: Can provide the wire or metal parts for trap triggers, snares or holders for cooking utensils.

COMBS: Their teeth can be broken off, sharpened and used as sewing needles.

PAIR OF TRAINERS: Shoes are essential for exploring inhospitable terrain or fishing in seawater. Laces can be used as rope and binding material.

BOOK OF MATCHES: Pray to God they didn't get wet. Conserve and keep for emergencies.

GLASSES: Emergency fire-lighting kit (remember Piggy in *Lord of the Flies*).

TEA BAGS: In cold temperatures keep for warming drink; in a hot climate keep dry, as can be used to alleviate sunburn.

PAPERBACK: If it's this book keep it. If it's a novel by Jeffery Archer use one page of purple prose at a time as kindling for fires. Keep all paper dry.

PAIR OF TIGHTS: Can be adapted to make netting for catching fish.

MAKEUP MIRROR: Use in sunlight to signal for help; put at bottom of stream to attract fish to your tights net.

STEREO HEADPHONES: Wires can be used for binding.

PINK PASHMINA: The colour doesn't matter; it's a carry-all sling, head protection and sun shelter.

BOTTLE OF VODKA: Tough call. Do you need the container more than the contents? Keep it for emergencies – medical emergencies. Hard liquor can be used as both anaesthetic and antiseptic.

Assess also what food you have with you, or, if you are very lucky, is hanging invitingly on a nearby tree. If you have water, always drink in small sips to maximise the effect of the fluid. If it is scarce, refrain from drinking to let your body get used to the new situation.

Conserve biscuits or dried food in sealed containers where possible, and keep food protected from flies and vermin. If you have freeze-dried or other dehydrated food with you, eat it only when you have enough water with you to digest it. Otherwise, it will just plug you up. You can survive without

food for much longer than you think. Do not make the mistake of eating any chocolate bars or snacks that you have with you. There may come a time when you need them – but it's not now.

One of your first priorities is to find more water. Make a quick scout around your camp looking for fresh water, but, if time and light are running short and you can't find any, don't worry. There are a number of simple tricks to collect water overnight.

Collecting water from a tree branch

Find a leafy green branch. Put a plastic bag around tree branches and tie it off (use a shoelace rather than the bag handles: you do not want to damage your precious bags). The mouth of the bag should be at the top with a corner hanging lower down. The moisture from the tree will condense in the bag over a few hours, yielding a few vital sips of water.

Tomorrow your first task is to find water.

When you're cast away, every day you survive is another victory. So far you're winning. Just get through the first night.

You may be stranded for a long time, but remember: **DON'T PANIC!**

SHIT HAPPENS! Small problems can become big problems; minor ailments must not be ignored

Blisters

When your survival depends on the ability to walk, don't underestimate the seriousness of blisters or the speed with which they can develop. Inspect your feet frequently for red patches. Apply plasters, if you have them, to these spots, or use anything soft, such as moss or leaves, to protect the skin from being rubbed by your boot or shoe. If you do develop blisters, do not burst them wide open; this multiplies the pain and increases the chance of infection. Instead, prick a few tiny holes around the edges of each swelling and very gently ease out the fluid through these pinpricks. Wait for the fluid to evaporate and apply a plaster before you continue walking.

A large blister on the sole of your foot may burst and get infected, making it hard to walk. To prevent this take a small sewing needle with some cotton thread. Sterilise the needle by holding it over an open flame until it turns black. Pass the needle and thread through the blister and out the other side. Remove the needle leaving two small ends of thread hanging out. The thread allows the fluid to drain out and dries out the blister without a huge hole in the skin. Do this at night. Try to keep the foot raised and by morning you should be able too walk without pain or breaking the skin.

Exhaustion

Rest and sleep are as essential to survival as anything. Health, morale, efficiency and intelligence all collapse if you're tired. Don't try to do everything at once. Pace yourself.

Exposure

Being cold is no fun. Cold and wet is even worse. When you are cold you become clumsy (as your blood deserts your fingers and toes to warm your core) and irritable, and you need to urinate all the time, leading to dehydration. Get dry; keep your head covered.

However warm the days, you need to have cover against rain and plunging nighttime temperatures. In cold and temperate climates without proper shelter you run the risk of hypothermia, when the body is unable to maintain normal temperature. Without adequate clothing or shelter, this can start at temperatures as high as 25ºC (77ºF). Shivering is the earliest sign, and should be a spur to immediate action. Then comes irrational behaviour and bursts of energy followed by lethargy. Someone who has become 'thermally incapable' can't touch their thumb to their little finger. It gets a lot worse. Get this person warm and dry!

Sunburn

When unprotected skin is exposed to the sun, the sun's beams penetrate the skin wall and start cooking the cells from the inside. Your skin cells don't like this, and react by drying out, getting inflamed, dying off or mutating into a ghastly cancer. The surrounding tissue does its best to help by flooding serum to the area to protect the damaged skin. In short, it blisters in the sun.

If two-thirds of your body is affected by sunburn blisters, it can kill you. Do not burst the blisters, but cover with dressings. For milder cases, if you do not have commercial aloe-based soothers, you could apply towels soaked in warm tea to the sunburned areas (the Maoris used a concoction made of the leaves of the manuka, one of several types of tea tree). The tannin in the tea heals the burn, and the tepid heat is much more comforting than cold water. The oils in milk and yoghurt also soothe burns.

The obvious advice is to avoid sunburn by taking sensible precautions. Commercial sunscreens should be used where available. Don't rub coconut water on yourself. You'll just smell like a piña colada. Coconut oil, useful for making your own sun cream and as a post-sun moisturizer, comes from the meat of the fruit once it has been dried, grated, heated with water, strained, then boiled for several hours.

As well as burned skin, too much sun can give heatstroke, which is very nasty even in a mild form, with hot dry skin, racing pulse and a headache from hell. Vomiting and unconsciousness can follow. Give your patient liquids and cool him with tepid water sprinkled on him as he lies in a shady, ventilated spot.

Cuts and scrapes

Scraping yourself along a piece of sharp coral is incredibly painful. Even a small cut in a vital place can make a hand, arm or leg unusable. Most dangerous of all is the risk of infection. Some corals are poisonous, and their hot and wet environment is a haven for bacteria, so cuts often become infected. You don't want to be amputating limbs just yet.

Get your hands as clean as possible before treating wounds. Remove any foreign bodies in the cut by thoroughly washing it in clean water. Always swab from the centre outwards. If the wound is already infected, soak in hot salty water for fifteen minutes, thoroughly drain of puss, then soak in clean salt water and cover. Garlic juice, thyme leaves and horseradish root are all good natural antiseptics. Apply a dressing if you have one and immobilise the wound in a comfortable position.

If you lack the equipment or clean water to clean and dress the wound thoroughly, it must be left open to heal from the inside. It will soon form a natural defence of its own. Don't panic: the human body, if well fed, is amazingly good at resisting and fighting infections.

Insect bites

Soldiers don't use soap, wash their hair or use antiperspirants or aftershave for at least three days before going into the jungle because it is the scent of these toiletries that attracts the mosquitoes. During summer the insect life in the northern forests is particularly vicious. Mosquitoes the size of small dogs (OK, not *that* big) can smell shampoo or perfume miles away and home in more effectively than a smart missile. Black flies are worse, a biblical plague of tiny flying sharks in swarms so thick they clog every available orifice.

To repel ticks, mosquitoes and black flies, try a diluted tincture of yarrow (*Achillea millefolium*) flowers directly on all exposed skin. A US Army study showed yarrow tincture to be more effective than DEET (diethyl toluamide) as an insect repellent. You can slap mud on your face and other bits of exposed skin if there is no other form of protection.

Every schoolkid knows that dock leaves ease the pain of stinging nettles. They also work for insect bites, but the plantain is even better. Also called *ribwort, pig's ear* and the *Band-Aid plant*, it is common in temperate areas around the world. You can identify it by the five parallel veins running the length of each leaf. (Most leaves have a central vein with smaller ones branching out from it.) Pick a leaf, chew it well and put it on the bite. The pain, heat and swelling, even allergic reactions, disappear, fast. (You can dry plantain leaves and carry them in your first-aid kit. Chew as you would fresh leaves.) Effective alternatives to plantain include comfrey, yellow dock, wild geranium, wild mallow, chickweed and yarrow.

In the woods, you can take a leaf from a tree, chew it and apply that to the bite. Any tree will do in an emergency, but the best leaves are witch hazel, willow, oak or maple. Play it safe: learn to recognise witch hazel and willow leaves before you chew on them. Maple or oak leaves are easier to recognise and safer to chew – unless you are where poison oak grows. If uncertain, avoid all shrubs and any trees with slick or shiny leaves. If the leaf you are chewing tastes extremely bitter or burns your mouth, spit it out at once.

Mud is the oldest and simplest poultice. Powdered white clay, which should be mixed with a little water or herb tea, can be applied directly to the sting as soon as possible. Finely ground grains such as rice and oatmeal, or bland, starchy substances such as mallow root, grated potato and arrowroot powder can also be used as soothing poultices to ease itching and pain from insect bites.

All these work for bee and other stings. Lemon juice and vinegar can also help in soothing horsefly and wasp stings. Fire ashes mixed with water to make a paste also works. Remove bee stingers carefully from the victim's flesh.

| 2 |  | ✂ | ! |

THE FIRST DAY

CASTAWAY

CASTAWAY

*'Christian died last – twice wounded; and once more
Mercy was offered when they saw his gore ...'*

Byron, 'The Island'

⚓ Liquid assets

Lush oases exist only in movies and the sun-blasted imagination. Without water you will be in serious trouble. Soon.

As our bodies are made up of 75 per cent water the effects of dehydration are fast and debilitating, starting with an ever-increasing lethargy. Even mild dehydration impairs concentration, which is dangerous at a time when clear thinking is essential. (Every time you pee, check the colour of your urine – dark yellow or brown indicates dehydration.) This is followed by severe headaches, joint pains and muscle cramps as the skin shrinks and the eyes sink into their sockets. Saliva thickens into a foaming, foul-tasting scum until you can no longer create any at all; then your tongue hardens and swells, squeezing past the jaws. Speech degenerates into inarticulate moans, hearing is affected and you begin to hallucinate.

It gets worse. Your still-living body starts a progressive mummification. The eyelids crack, eyeballs weep tears of blood and the throat is so swollen that breathing becomes difficult – so difficult that in a horrible twist of fate you believe you are drowning. Should you survive that long, the body then enters the phase of living death. The skin resembles blackened leather, cuts bleed dry, the lips disappear, exposing teeth and gums while the nose withers to half its size.

Dying of thirst is no way to go.

A normal, adult, healthy male needs about 3.5 litres (6 pints) of water a day. You can survive on about 0.6 litre (1 pint) a day, but no less. In the tropics the minimum that the body needs to function is 1.1 litres (2 pints). Don't ration your water below this level – castaways have been found dead of dehydration with their water tanks half full.

If you have to ration water, divide it into several small portions over the day. Hold the water in your mouth as long as you can, then gargle before swallowing. This will rehydrate the tissues in your mouth and make you feel less thirsty.

Usually, about half the water you consume comes back out, half as urine, a quarter as sweat and a quarter as water vapour from the lungs. The first day, drink no water at all, however much you want to. This will cause your body to activate its water-saving techniques, including reducing urination. You now need less water to survive. After the first day, you should start drinking your pint a day.

If you have no water, *do not* eat. Your body uses up water to process food. Make sure you keep an eye on others for any signs of water deprivation.

When you find a fresh water supply after a period of dehydration resist the temptation to knock it back like an Aussie sheep shearer quaffing his first beer after a hard day with the clippers. Chances are you'll end up throwing it straight back up, losing valuable liquid and polluting your new supply in one relch.

Don't risk running out of water before you try to find more. Choose the right time to explore your surroundings – early morning is best, when it is cooler – and be logical in the way you search. Make sure, if you are exploring, that you drink plenty of fluid before setting out and, if possible, take some with you.

Ration your sweat, not your water

If it is extremely hot do not remove your clothing, since your sweat will evaporate more quickly and you will dehydrate faster. If you are overheating, stop and rest. If you are already suffering from dehydration, bear in mind that it makes it easier for you to get tired, confused or lost in unknown territory. Make sure you leave enough time to get back to camp before nightfall.

How to find water

Ideally, you want to find running water because that can, *in extremis*, be drunk without having to be boiled. Fast-running water is generally safer than large slow-moving rivers. The colder water is, the more likely it is to be safe.

Look for signs or sources of water at the bottoms of valleys, in gullies or dry stream beds. Lush vegetation growing out of cliffs indicates a water source. In mountains or sea cliffs look for pools of water in natural hollows and crevices. On, or near a beach, digging a hole for water might produce some that is salty. But the fresh water will float to the top, from where it can be spooned off.

Grazing animals and grain-eating birds drink at dawn and dusk. Look for tracks leading downhill and birds flying straight and low (when birds have drunk their fill they fly from tree to tree, stopping frequently for a rest) and follow them. If you spot them in the evening, make a note of the direction and aim to follow it as the sun rises.

When you find a pool with water running into it, follow the stream upriver for up to a little over a kilometre (half a mile) to make sure that there are no animal corpses polluting the stream. If you find one, pull it out and continue upstream.

No-nos

Just because you've found a pool of water, it doesn't mean it's safe to drink. The US Environmental Protection Agency estimates that 90 per cent of the world's fresh water is unsafe without treatment. The main ways water gets contaminated is by agricultural and industrial pollution (which if you're lost is probably a good sign that 'civilisation' is close at hand).

If the ground around the pool is covered in foam, leave it alone. Water does not foam unless it has been heavily contaminated. Do not drink it. One exception to this is in lagoons or pools at the bottom of jungle waterfalls. The foam there may be caused by the constant churning of the water reacting with the tannins from jungle foliage.

Generally, it is a bad idea to drink sitting water. Stagnant pools are collection points for everything that can possibly be washed into them. Since the only way these pools can empty is through evaporation, the concentration of contaminants endlessly increases. A pool with no greenery but an assortment of animal bones around the edges is most likely polluted. Don't touch the water, but take the bones for use as tools. Other danger signs are: lack of insect life; absence of animals or animal tracks; a white coating on the rocks or ground around the water.

In some areas springs can have a dangerously high alkaline content leeched from minerals. Alkali-tainted water is bitter and leaves a long aftertaste in the mouth, so it is easily identified. Smelling the water will give you an early indication of whether it is drinkable. One test of the freshness of water is to wiggle your finger in your ear and pull out a bit of wax. Drop this in the water: if it sinks, the water is fresh. If the water is questionable, the wax will form an oily sheen on the surface.

Any water that comes from a pool with no obvious run-in and run-off must always be boiled before drinking. Filter it as well – through a T-shirt or, better still, a filter made from a sock, with alternate layers of charcoal and sand. To sterilise the water, boil for five minutes, plus an extra minute for every thousand feet above sea level. It makes the water taste flat, but that can be remedied by pouring it from one container to another a few times, which re-oxygenates it, speeds the cooling process and puts the flavour back.

If the water looks bad but you must drink right now, pull a piece of cloth over your mouth and put your face down in the water and suck. This will filter out at least some of the impurities.

✎ Should I stay or should I go?

The answer to this question is usually to stay close to where you first landed or crashed or however you arrived at this place. It doesn't mean you have to stay sleeping under that makeshift roof of branches on a rotten log inhabited by extra-sociable termites. But remember that search parties always start at the last known location of the missing party and move out from there in ever-increasing circles. If you've survived a shipwreck or plane crash, you should remain as close as possible to any visible wreckage.

If you're in a place where you are in physical danger – an exposed spit or where wild animals threaten – then move to the nearest safe location. When you do, make a note or marks on the trees and ground showing the direction you went in.

Before leaving, take stock and evaluate your chances. Do you know where and how far you will have to travel? Do you know what the terrain is like? Is the weather good or bad?

If you stay put, do you have any food or water? How long will it last? Is your position sheltered and warm? If so, it may be wiser to stay where you are than risk a long trek through burning sun or freezing snow. If you stay you may face eventual starvation; if you set out, you will exhaust your reserves of energy much faster, especially if anyone is hurt.

What about rescue? Does anyone know where you are? If so, how long will it take them to come looking for you? And will they know where to search? Is your current position easily visible from the air?

Questions, nothing but questions. But it is important you answer them rationally, and that the decision is agreed by everybody.

When you're not alone

So how was that decision reached?

If you are cast away with others, how you make collective decisions could make the difference between surviving and not. It will determine not only how good those decisions are, but also the very essence of the group. We humans can help others one moment and become aggressive and unco-operative the next. Some groups flourish while others dissolve into violent anarchy.

People power

More people means more ideas, more workers and more expertise. But it's more than many hands making light work. The essential resource of a group lies in its differences. Every member of the group will bring something to the collective nobody else can.

Interaction is the lifeblood of all groups. People talk to each other, relate their experiences, watch each other, and sometimes touch. Through interaction, they may come to recognise that they are not as different, isolated or as incompetent as they had thought. The group nourishes and protects the individual. The strong can help the weak, thereby boosting their own confidence and feeling of worth. In all, the whole can be greater than the sum of the parts.

On a primeval level, we need other people, or more precisely their reactions to us, to confirm we exist. Which is why solitary confinement – or even shunning people – is such an effective and damaging punishment. It undermines your very identity as human.

SHIT HAPPENS! Group self-destruction: Pitcairn Island

The *Bounty* was on its way from Tahiti to the Caribbean, carrying breadfruit seedlings, when on the morning of 28 April 1789, twelve crew members, led by Master's Mate Fletcher Christian, staged a mutiny, taking over the ship and setting Lieutenant William Bligh and eighteen of his supporters adrift in the vessel's launch.

The mutineers then set out to find a hideaway island where they could live out their lives away from the world. After much searching, Christian, along with eight mutineers, six Polynesian men, twelve women and one baby, reached remote, rocky, inhospitable Pitcairn Island on 15 January 1790. 'With a joyful expression such as we had not seen on him for a long time past', Christian returned from the shore to report that the people who had once planted Pitcairn with coconut palms and breadfruit had either died or left. The island was lonely, uninhabited, fertile and warm; it exceeded his highest hopes.

The *Bounty* was anchored in what is now called Bounty Bay and stripped of all her contents, including pigs, chickens, yams and sweet potatoes, which were laboriously hauled up the aptly named Hill of Difficulty to The Edge, a small, grassy platform overlooking the Bay. Fearing that if any European vessel sighted the ship retribution would inevitably follow, the mutineers ran the *Bounty* ashore and set her on fire so that no trace of her would remain visible from the sea.

The mutineers made rough leaf shelters, and quickly realised that the island could provide for pretty much all their material needs. But within three years there had been a serious revolt by the women, suppressed with difficulty, and then Christian was murdered by the Polynesian men, angered at their treatment as virtual slaves.

In the ensuing bloodbath all of the Polynesian men were slaughtered and three other mutineers also lost their lives.

These early years were characterised by chaos. 'They didn't really set up any kind of society,' says Herbert Ford, director of the Pitcairn Island Study Center, based in California, in an interview with the BBC. 'They were all chiefs – they had guns and they had women. The Polynesian men they brought with them were treated very much as slaves and this master-servant society soon led to trouble – bloodshed became a way of life.'

Things got even worse when one of the men, who had once worked in a distillery, discovered how to brew a potent spirit from the roots of the ti plant (*Cordyline terminalis* or *australis*), also known as the cabbage tree. Murders and drownings followed, and by 1800 the adult male population of the island had dwindled to just one.

Grouchos and lynch mobs

'I don't want to belong to any club that will accept me as a member.'

Groucho Marx

We all know well-behaved kids who become little hooligans when with their mates. Peer pressure, of course. The more you need to join the club, the greater the pressure the club can exert on you. In a castaway community where the need for acceptance is almost absolute, even Groucho might feel compelled to break his rule.

Membership of a group is a tug of war between compromise and constraint. Some people are Grouchos who prefer to mutter under their breaths about cooks who spoil the broth, or the perils of design by committee.

But if someone rejects the aims and methods of the group, they can be quickly ostracised and isolated, weakening the group overall. Somehow you're no longer 'all in the same boat'.

But the 'united we stand at all costs' approach has hidden dangers. Everyone's been with a group of mates arguing about where to go on Saturday night and ended up in a crap place that nobody likes. That's groupthink not working properly. No wants to rock the boat by disagreeing, but achieving a consensus with the least conflict is not always the correct path.

All groups develop codes of behaviour. In an isolated community, while shared 'civilised' and moral standards provide an initial structure, other social rules can be modified. For example, on a tropical island casual nudity might be acceptable to all. However, deeper changes to the norm can also occur, leading to extreme behaviour. A recent trial of six male leaders in Pitcairn Island unearthed a culture in which underage sex had been accepted, if not condoned, for generations.

The culture and character of a group is determined by its personalities and the circumstances in which it is formed. Individuals' views of the group may oscillate between enchantment – when, for instance, the group inspires them to take on something they thought beyond their ability – and disillusionment. Life in groups can produce creativity, energy, productivity and satisfaction, but this is often punctuated by frustration, hostility, compromise, slowness and periods of breakdown. Such ups and downs are normal and should be expected.

Another major danger is 'contagion'. We've all been swept along by a group of people surfing on the tide of high emotions. That's how riots start and lynch mobs form. Once the emotion has worn off individuals can be horrified by their behaviour, but by then it's too late. Contagion is one reason groups tend to take riskier decisions than individuals.

It is worth remembering this if the decision is a matter of life or death. The more you understand about how groups work, the better. Everyone might agree that the 'group interest' is to be warm and fed, but it is when someone wants to be *warmer* and *better* fed than someone else that troubles really start. Tim, who can't, or won't, eat fish might suggest that the group spend days hunting for meat instead. If they don't catch anything, that means everyone goes hungry (not in the group interest) and Tim is not popular (which is not in either Tim's or the group's interest).

Stormin' Norman's forming but not performing

Be prepared for a rocky start. Most groups go through four distinct phases of development.

1. FORMING: A time of anxiety and a need for a leader. Thrown into a new and alien environment where old rules no longer apply, people don't know how to behave. Lost sheep need somebody to tell them what to do. In the West, we are brought up to consider ourselves as unique individuals, as islands. This social distance ensures that we feel in control of our lives and that the other islands visit only in well-understood ways and when allowed to do so. As the group 'forms', everyone's checking everyone else out. There are instant chemical reactions – 'I like Jack but there's something about Danni I don't trust' – jockeying for position and judgements made. No one shows their true self.

2. STORMING: I'm not a number: I'm a free man! Guards are still up, initial reactions and prejudices remain, but the desire to find consensus wanes. Sheep start to make their opinions known, some rebel against the rules. Competition between subgroups – which team can find the most food today? – while productive in the short term might be planting the seeds for later conflict.

3. NORMING: Co-operation is beautiful, man. Norms of acceptable behaviour are established, and mutual 'group' interest agreed. Resistance to the group is overcome, conflicts patched up, there is a group cohesion and hugs and kisses now mean more than just mutual support. People start to reveal who they really are and are prepared to admit earlier impressions may have been wrong.

4. PERFORMING: You've made it. This is the place you want to be, where squabbles are resolved, people know where they sit, their roles are flexible and functional, their energy is focused. The hard part, as everyone knows, is to keep performing. A group may achieve cohesion only to slip back into storming mode if circumstances change

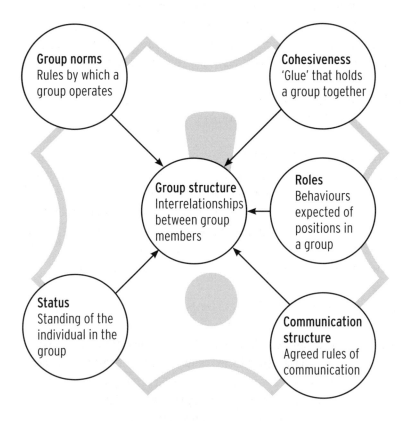

Group norms
Rules by which a group operates

Cohesiveness
'Glue' that holds a group together

Group structure
Interrelationships between group members

Roles
Behaviours expected of positions in a group

Status
Standing of the individual in the group

Communication structure
Agreed rules of communication

Five components of group structure which affect performance, stability and effectiveness of a group

Decisions, decisions

How quickly your group starts performing is down to how you make key decisions early on. The moment the first person says, 'Let's discuss what to do' someone will probably dispute whether that is in the 'group interest'. Start with agreeing on how to make decisions and how to resolve conflict. Don't wait for the first argument – that could well be too late.

So, how are you as a group going to make decisions? Does every member have an equal say, or do 'experts' decide some issues? Should those who have actually built something form a 'shelter committee' to make key decisions without recourse to the others? If it is to be a genuinely 'group verdict' on major choices, is this decided by consensus or majority decision, or does it have to be unanimous? Or is the decision made by one leader?

It is already getting prickly. Do you need a leader, and, if so, who? How should the leader be appointed? What are their functions?

The leader of the pack

Robinson Crusoe rescues Man Friday, and the latter is already on his knees and kissing the ground in gratitude before they even communicate. Soon, Crusoe, the self-appointed 'prince and lord of the whole island', has Friday named, addressing him as 'Master' and working in his small cornfield under his direction. Fine for Crusoe, but perhaps not so good for Friday, who isn't allowed to eat human flesh any more, let alone worship his own god.

At the beginning of William Golding's *Lord of the Flies*, the classic parable of castaway group behaviour, the schoolboys meet to decide what to do. Ralph, who had blown a conch shell to call the meeting, announces, 'Seems to me we ought to have a chief to decide things.' This suggestion is agreed by acclaim. Jack says it should be him because he is 'chapter chorister and head boy. I can sing C sharp!' Someone suggests a vote. Jack secures the vote of his subgroup, the choristers, but the others go for Ralph, because of his 'stillness ... his size and attractive appearance; and most obscurely, yet most powerfully, there was the conch'.

CASTAWAY

By blowing the conch to call the scattered boys together for a meeting, Ralph had shown himself to be able to take control of situations. By suggesting and winning a leadership contest, he had demonstrated his ability to influence the behaviour of others. These are two traditional characteristics of leaders. He does less well when he gifts his rival Jack control of the choir, thus cementing their status as a potentially rebellious subgroup, and showing his own fatal weakness for following the line of least resistance.

Leadership, like belonging and 'joining', gives a lot of people the shivers. The army, businesses and schools have found that having a clear hierarchy is conducive to efficiency. This works only when there is some degree of reward or threat backing up compliance with group rules. In less formal or random groups, leaders can emerge, be acclaimed or, like Ralph, be elected by majority vote. However, they must carry the majority of the group with them by force of argument.

Decision making by popular vote has one clear advantage in that it leads to higher levels of involvement and commitment. But, for this to work, a number of factors need to be in place. First, all members of the group need to have access to all the information available; there has to be sufficient time to consider various options and the potential consequences; trust must exist among group members; and there has to be a process in place to deal with unhelpful behaviour and manipulative or dominant individuals.

For there to be trust, hidden motivations must be outed. Everyone must agree on and understand the goals of the group. But, before you commit to this, you must feel that you have had your say. This demands a culture where listening is important and people are open to one another's feelings.

If ideas are to be freely expressed and considered as potential solutions, you can't rely on people's better nature. You need – *gasp!* – Rules of Procedure. Not the archaic nonsense of the House of Commons or the law

courts, but something to prevent shouting matches or only the loudest being heard. Perhaps there should be an hour every day, with people being allowed to speak for only ten minutes. It would be like a committee. But a committee needs a chairperson.

We're back with leadership again.

Leadership needn't be all about the inequality of *Robinson Crusoe* or the power struggles of *Lord of the Flies*. In Japan groups are often constructed around cohesion and a clear, undisputed leader whose responsibility is to be sensitive to the wellbeing of both the group and individual group members. So the 'leader' of a consensual castaway group of equals has a clear and strictly limited role: to manage the interaction of the group so that minority feelings are allowed to be expressed, even if that just means enforcing a time limit on expression or calming threatening behaviour.

A group that can establish a problem-solving and decision-making structure is well on the way to performing. You should also take steps actively to shape the group's culture as it emerges. Encourage everyone to acknowledge their feelings and problems and to support each other. The trust and closeness you build while 'forming' can forge bonds to see you through bad times. If group members feel that their concerns are ignored or their feelings dismissed, the opposite may occur.

When you meet, sit in a circle. It represents equality and democracy, but allows everyone to see everyone else. Some groups develop mantras: 'Everyone who is here belongs here just because he is here and for no other reason'; 'Our first purpose is to make contact with each other – everything else we might want or need comes second'.

Everyone needs to have a high level of commitment to the group. To achieve this, stress your shared objectives, and keep reminding yourself that the future of the whole group is the responsibility of each member.

Tinker, Tailor ... Cook

On a more practical level, you should discover and weigh up the skills that individuals possess. Some will be stronger, more practical or more co-ordinated. Some will be able to sew, some to sail, some to saw. If you have an expert on something and people to spare, allot an understudy to learn from them so that in the case of disaster their expertise is not lost.

Other vital group skills may be less obvious. More subtle roles are adopted without anyone planning, or even noticing it at first. Someone might be a good listener, to whom members of the group turn when in distress. Someone else might be a great motivator, driving the group to more energetic or speedy achievements. Appreciate and encourage these differences, for they are the secret to a successful group.

Less specialised tasks must be shared out fairly, especially if they are onerous, boring or unpleasant. Equality is all. Without it, whatever mantras they may be chanting, the group is doomed.

It is also important to set up routines because they take the unpredictability out of the confusing and dislocating experience. Certain jobs – collecting wood, picking seaweed or beachcombing – need to be done every day. Wherever possible, two people should be assigned to a task. But not the same two people every time – this keeps the interaction going. For the first few nights, guard should be kept in two-person, four-hour shifts. Their job is to be alert for potential predators and to keep the home fires burning.

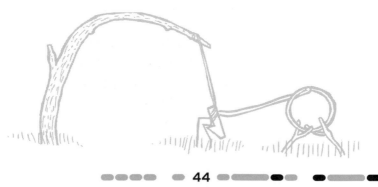

⚓ Looking around

Having started the process of becoming a group, you now need to find a permanent home. First, assess the environment in the immediate vicinity of your first-night camp. Is it safe? Where is the nearest water supply? What food can you forage within a ten-minute walk? Send two-person teams along the seashore in opposite directions and at least one team inland. Their task is to reconnoitre and report back within a set time. They are looking for fresh water, food sources, better camp sites and human and animal signs.

If you find something useful – an old crate, a plastic bottle – pull it off the shore and pick it up on the way back. Check out rock pools, looking for shellfish and different types of seaweed. If you're not sure whether they are edible, bring a small sample back. Check out caves and mark as a possible storm shelter. If the sand is damp inside and there is no sign of fresh water coming in it probably floods at high tide, which is not what you want.

You are going to have to shit in the woods but, when you have done your business, dig a small hole and cover it up. Until you know more about your environment, do not advertise your presence in it and do not despoil it.

Back at the site, think about rescue. Find the best location close by for a signalling fire, and stockpile wood near it. Three fires in a triangle is an internationally recognised distress signal. If there is a large expanse of sandy beach write out 'SOS' or 'HELP' in giant letters using stones.

Survival essentials

KNIFE: The Swiss Army knife is a wonderful invention, though current airline regulations mean you can't carry it on as hand luggage. The top-end model has so many attachments (it weighs 2 kilos (4.4 pounds) and has 500 blades) that you need a manual to understand it all – and they are a bit bulky. Twenty quid buys a basic, cover-most-minor-emergencies knife, but do make sure it has scissors and also a corkscrew, should you be thinking of laying down some fine vintage wines for later.

You should also seriously consider the Leatherman and Gerber range of multitools. These contain very strong pliers, saw blades, wire cutters and a variety of blades and screwdrivers. The scissors on the Mini Leatherman are excellent. If you own a multitool, either wear it on a belt pouch or attach to a lanyard so you don't lose it.

Beware of cheap knock-off Swiss Army knives and multitools – they talk the talk but can't cut the bark. Blades go blunt fast or snap off. Avoid as you would a spitting cobra.

Given a choice you'd be better off considering a sheath knife, an all-purpose, stronger survival tool. Don't underestimate the psychological effect of having a knife strapped to your belt. Whatever you feel inside, it says 'confident, macho, hunter and woodsman' to everybody except predators with especially large teeth and sharp claws. The blade should be one-sided and at least as long as your extended palm. 10–15cm (4–6 inches) is ideal: small enough for intricate work but also long enough to work on branches. Carbon steel is better than stainless steel at holding an edge (keep it sharp enough so you can shave with it) and you can use the blunt edge as

the striker with flint to make fire. The metal of the blade must extend the length of the knife, and the handle, ideally the width of your palm to reduce blisters, should be treated wood or other comfortable water-resistant material.

The pommel of the handle must be tough enough to withstand repeated pounding. Don't bother with a guard between blade and handle as they get in the way.

Finally, before buying a bush knife, test it's strong enough. Drive the blade 4cm (1.5 inches) into a tree at right angles to the grain. Stand on the handle. If it breaks, you don't want it!

Axe (or how the West was won): To a true woodsman his axe is more important than his knife. With an axe comes control. You are not reliant on fallen logs and dead wood. Trees can be cut down, shaped and trimmed for building roofs, houses, boats and masts. Be very careful when you use an axe. Wood is harder to cut through than bone and sinew.

There are three basic sizes of axe. The small camp axe or hatchet has a handle of about 30cm (1 foot) and is the most dangerous to use, since it can end up embedded in your knee or bouncing off the forehead. The general-purpose axe is the favoured size for wilderness survivalists. Hold the head in your hand and the handle should rest in your armpit. Careless use can result in loss of toes. The large axe has a handle about a metre (3 feet 3 inches) long and is the safest, since the head usually ends up in the ground rather than a limb.

Using an axe properly and economically takes a lot of practice. Keep the axe head sharp (a minute's sharpening saves five minutes' chopping) and look after it. With an axe you can build a civilisation. Without one you are left trying to survive until civilisation finds you.

Survival tin (with this you can survive)

Old-fashioned, flat, two-ounce tobacco tins are very popular because they fit easily into a pocket. You can buy metal containers with a screw top or canvas pouches, but make sure that, whatever you use, the contents will remain dry. A round boiled-sweetie tin will not do. If you shape your materials into rectangles you can pack in a lot more than you think. Two strips of duct tape will keep it shut. Or use thick rubber bands, which can be adapted to use in a catapult. Polish the inside of the lid to act as a signalling reflector.

MATCHES/CANDLE: Shave the candle down. Melt the shaved wax into a puddle and dip match heads in it to keep them waterproof. Scrape off wax when you want to strike. Non-safety matches are best.

FLINT AND STEEL: For when the matches run out. Practise with it when you have a moment.

NEEDLES AND STRONG THREAD: Get a selection of needle sizes up to a sail maker's needle with a large eye that will take thicker sinew. You may need to sew sailcloth or animal hides together. Wrap thread around needles to keep them together.

FISH HOOKS AND THIN NYLON LINE: Hooks have a habit of getting lost or embedding themselves into fleshy bits. Treat with care but keep safe. Add a few little sinkers (lead balls to weigh hook down), and a minimum 30 metres (about 100 feet) of thin line to your hooks.

COMPASS: Liquid-filled with luminous button.

WATER-PURIFYING TABLETS: One tablet handles a litre of water.

Don't use more than you need to, since they taste nasty and, anyway, you may need them.

WATERPROOF PLASTERS/BUTTERFLY SUTURES: You might prefer to take a strip of waterproof plaster and cut off what you need, but it still needs to be kept dry and sterile. Sutures will close wounds and are a lot less painful than getting out the needle and thread.

MINI-TORCH/BETA LIGHT: Something small and light with long-lasting batteries for those stumble-into-camp-late moments. Beta lights contain light-emitting crystals that can also be used to attract fish at night.

SURGICAL BLADES/HARD-BACKED RAZORBLADES: Keep them sterile in their foil packaging. Hard-backed razorblades are easier to grip. Don't blunt blades by trying to cut stuff they can't handle – such as tree trunks.

FLEXIBLE SAW: A specialist survival tool. Approximately 60cm (2 feet) long and made from eight strands of stainless-steel wire, this is big enough to saw through big logs (when they're on the ground!), plastics, metal and, if absolutely necessary, bone. Thumbs go in the rings at each end, and you must saw slowly to avoid overheating the metal. Also doubles as a snare and a most unpleasant garrotte.

SNARE WIRE: 60–90cm (2–3 feet) of brass wire.

SURVIVAL BAG, LIGHTWEIGHT PLASTIC SHEET OR PONCHO: Probably too big to fit in the tin, but make sure you can find space for it somewhere, because it has a myriad uses. Provided you do actually want to be found, bright orange is a nice colour and will catch the eye of a rescue party more easily than camouflage will.

CASTAWAY

Condoms: No sex – just water carriers. A condom will hold a litre of water without bursting.

Whistle: Make sure it's flat, plastic and noisy. Good way of keeping in touch with people in thick bush and of attracting rescuers.

Nylon cord: As thin and as strong as you can find. Pack as much as you can fit: 15 metres (50 feet) minimum. Parachute cord has a breaking strain of 250kg (550 pounds).

Cotton wool/tampons: To pack everything in so it doesn't rattle and move about. Do not use to remove makeup. Tampons (remove applicator) are made from very fine cotton wool and when charred make brilliant tinder for lighting fires. In medical emergencies use to clean wounds.

Magnifying glass: Can be used to light fires.

Pencil and paper: You may want to draw maps, or keep or leave notes.

Zip-loc plastic bag: Keeps things dry and can be used to collect water.

Solar-powered iPod: Dream on!

ADAPT TO SURVIVE

CASTAWAY

CASTAWAY

Being cast away is a great diet. It's called starvation. Surviving off the land can be like eating celery (legend has it that you consume more calories eating celery than it gives you back). On average, our bodies use 1,700 calories every day just to stay alive; if we're exercising hard in an extreme environment we can burn more than 5,500 calories. You need to keep up your calorie intake to balance the amount you're burning, so spending hours every day finding and preparing food that may not provide enough calories is potentially dangerous.

We replace calories by eating carbohydrates, fat and protein. One gram of protein (meat, fish, eggs, nuts, grains and pulses) and 1 gram of carbs (sugars and starches) each produces 4 calories. One gram of fat produces 9 calories. So, if you're cast away, throw away the perceived wisdom that governs eating habits in the West – fat is now an essential part of your diet. The body also requires vitamins, trace elements and minerals.

Everything you need to survive may be available to you but not at the same time. Seasons affect what's harvestable and meat and fish do not keep indefinitely, so you have to be prepared to swing between feast and famine or graze as you move about, eating little and often. The best storage facility is the stomach, which processes food into fuel and keeps you going until you can collect more food. Hunger pangs fade after a day or two. Weakness and dizziness gradually become more severe, but survival for up to a month without any food intake is not unusual. Don't panic if you haven't found as much food as you think you need.

If it grows, walks, crawls, swims, flies, scuttles or limps you can probably eat it. Something already is.

There is plenty to gather by foraging on the beach, or in the woods. Don't start by hunting a wild pig when you can get by on seaweed, shellfish, bugs, termites, worms, slugs, snails and, though they might prove a little harder to source, puppy-dog tails. All you need is a stick for digging, something to carry what you find and the ability to eat your catch without throwing up.

Sea shore

Start at the beach. Slightly inland might be salt marshes and mangroves, home to mud crabs and mud snails. Cockles and pipi (an edible shellfish) can be dug up in sandier sediments beyond the mangroves. If the shore is rocky, look for lichens, at mid-shore for small acorn barnacles, oysters and turfing seaweed. At the low-tide mark gather larger seaweeds such as kelp.

Check cracks in the rocks, pools and sea caves for shore crabs, stalked barnacles, sea anemones and whelks. Sea urchins are easy to spot and, if you're gentle, easy to gather: push them off the rock with a knife or stick and let them float gently into your palm; to eat, crack open the base and scoop out the orange roe, which is delicious.

Look for big waves crashing over rocks. There you will find encrusted species such as large acorn barnacles, mussels and a greater variety of large bushy seaweeds. Subtidal reefs provide excellent habitat for crabs, crayfish and red rock lobsters. They are easier to catch at night.

When collecting mussels and oysters, take precautions. Shellfish poisoning is violent and unpleasant and, while not usually fatal, will leech your body of liquid, vital minerals and vitamins. Avoid picking shellfish at a 'red tide', which in the daytime is a dull red, and at night makes the sea bioluminescent.

Don't pick mussels unless they are covered with seawater every day. Check if an open mussel is still alive by tapping the shell with a knife. If it doesn't close bin it. When you debeard it by yanking the tuft of seaweed from the undershell it should react. Before cooking, check there are no closed shells filled with mud that will taint the whole batch. When they have been boiled – not for too long, because the meat shrivels and loses its flavour – all the shells should be open. Discard any that haven't opened.

Cockles, winkles and whelks have a built-in trapdoor that closes if they are shaken. Boil them and extract the flesh using a pin, a sliver of bamboo or a sharpened hardwood twig. There is a knack to opening oysters raw by

inserting a knife blade under the lip on the underside of the shell. However, this is also a really good way of blunting or snapping off your knife blade. Better to steam or boil them, as the shell opens much easier when they are dead.

Seaweed

Seaweed is a great source of vitamins and fibre, which make it nutritious if not nourishing. It is about half cellulose, which humans cannot digest. While a few threadlike or slender branching seaweeds contain acids that can irritate your stomach, standard broad-leafed varieties are safe. Most are rich in minerals, containing between seven and fourteen times the calcium of milk, while 10–20 per cent of their dry weight is protein.

The Maori ate kelp, gigartina (a marine alga), purple laver and sea lettuce. Eat seaweed only if you have enough fresh water to rinse it thoroughly. If you have to wait until it rains, don't worry, as it dries nicely in the meantime.

Seaweed can be eaten cooked (stir briskly in hot water and then remove) or raw as a salad. It combines brilliantly with other ingredients, though you can simply boil up a sheet of dried kelp in water to make stock to which can be added flakes of dried fish. Put water over a medium heat and remove the kelp just before boiling.

Beware one poisonous creature that looks like seaweed. Stinging seaweed is actually a hydroid, related to the sea anemone. It grows only a few centimetres high, and is found on the sea floor, usually on coral reefs, in tropical waters.

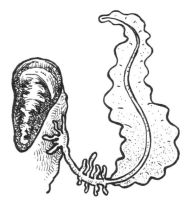

Kelp can be eaten and is a good source of key nutrients

Raupo – Maori Miracle Plant

Raupo (*Typha orientalis*) is a bog plant that looks like a large bulrush, and which grows throughout New Zealand. It has creeping rhizomes (underground stems), which give off long, linear leaves up to 2.5 metres (8 feet) tall. The minute pinkish brown flowers are crowded in spikes at the top of tall, rounded stems.

Next to the harakeke, raupo was probably the plant most used by the Maori. The pollen is rich in oils, carbohydrates and protein. Flower stalks with ripe pollen were collected in the early morning and put out in the sun to dry. The pollen was stripped off the top of the flower stalk and sifted to separate out the down. The resulting bright-yellow residue resembles mustard powder.

The pollen was mixed with water by the Wairoa Maori to make a porridge called rerepe. However, it was more common to use the pollen-water mixture to make pungapunga cakes, which were placed in leaf-lined baskets and cooked in an earth oven. The cakes are a solid mass of bright yellow and taste sweetish and light. The Tuhoe tribe also mixed the pollen with large quantities of crushed green manuka beetles, the mixture being steamed in a hangi (earth oven).

Entire young flowering stems can be eaten raw, cooked or made into a soup. It tastes a little like sweet corn. The seed is small and fiddly, but has a pleasant nutty taste when roasted and can yield an edible oil. The Maori also ate the springtime leaves and shoots after they had been cooked in an earth oven. Raupo, when eaten in springtime, allegedly acts as an aphrodisiac.

The roots of the raupo were dug up from swamp mud, peeled (to reveal their edible core high in carbohydrates) and eaten raw or cooked. Containing 30–45 per cent starch, raupo roots compare favourably with wheat, corn and rice. Eaten raw, they are mild, cooling, refreshing and pleasant. However they do have a high fibre content, and so need chewing before the residue is spat out.

The roots can also be boiled and eaten like potatoes or macerated and then boiled to yield a sweet syrup. They can also be dried, ground into a powder and used as a thickener in soups or added to cereal flours. Rich in protein, this flour is used to make biscuits, bread and cakes.

Medicinal uses

The dried pollen is an anticoagulant, but when roasted with charcoal it has the opposite properties and can be used internally to treat tapeworms, diarrhoea, kidney stones, haemorrhage, painful menstruation, postpartum pains, abscesses and cancer of the lymphatic system. It should not be given to pregnant women. Externally, it is used in the treatment of injuries.

Other uses

The stems have many uses. Gathered in the autumn, they make a good thatch and can be woven into mats, chairs, hats and so on. A good source of biomass, they make an excellent addition to the compost heap or can be used as a source of fuel. After harvesting the abundant plant, Maori women scraped the leaves with a sharp stone or shell to expose the inner fibres. These fibres would then be cleaned, prepared and woven, dyed and braided into mats, baskets, rope, fishing nets and piupiu skirts for dancing. A fibre obtained from the leaves can also be used for making paper.

The leaves are harvested in summer, autumn or winter and are soaked in water for 24 hours prior to cooking. The fibres are cooked for two hours with soda ash and then beaten in a ball mill for an hour and a half.

A fibre obtained from the roots can be used for making string. The hairs of the fruits are used for stuffing pillows. They have good insulating and buoyancy properties and can be used as a wound dressing and a lining for babies' nappies. The stems can be used to make rush lights. The outer skin is removed, except for a small strip, or spine, running the entire length to give stability. The stem is then soaked in oil. The pollen is highly flammable, can be used in making fireworks and will serve as tinder for fire making.

Music

The most famous Maori use of the raupo was in making *poi* balls, which are both percussion and dance instruments. Maori women use the poi to imitate the sounds, actions and rhythms of nature in their dances and songs and to enhance storytelling. Poi dances utilize either single or double short poi balls with cords about 20–25cm

(8–10 inches) long, or single or double long poi with cords about 65–90 (about 25–35 inches) long. Originally, poi balls were made of dried moss wrapped with raupo, which produced deep and distinctive tones as they hit the person's wrists or arms.

⚘ Plants and fruits

There will always be a plant, or part of a plant, you can eat. However just because animals eat something does not make it safe for you. Cows eat grass but it won't keep a human alive. Just over half of plant species are inedible or actually poisonous, so before trying something follow this simple test. It does not work on fungi.

The poison tester

Rub the plant on a sensitive area of skin, such as the inner wrist, to see if a reaction occurs. Crush the leaves. If there is a smell of peaches or bitter almonds, avoid.

If they get the thumbs-up, place a small portion on your lips. Wait 15 seconds. Place a small portion in the corner of your mouth. Wait again for the same time. Place a small portion on the tip of your tongue. Wait. Chew a small portion. If at any time you experience a sharp, stinging or burning feeling, indeed any discomfort, throw it away. Swallow a small amount and wait five hours. Don't eat or drink anything else in that time. If no reactions are experienced, you can consider the plant safe to eat.

If you do have an upset stomach, drink hot water, and don't eat again until the pain has gone. If the discomfort is severe, try to induce vomiting.

Plants you shouldn't eat

- Anything that looks like a bean, cucumber, melon or parsnip, with foliage that looks like dill, parsley, parsnips or carrots.
- Any plant that has orange, yellow, red, dark, or soapy-tasting sap, or sap that turns black after being exposed to air.
- Any plant that has a milky sap, with the exception of dandelions, wild figs and papayas.
- The seeds of fruits.
- Mushrooms you find in the wild — unless you are 100 per cent sure. They don't have enough food value to justify the risk.
- Any plant with umbrella-shaped blossoms.
- Any fruit that is in five sections.
- Plants with a three-leaved growth pattern.
- Grain heads with pink, purple or black spurs.
- Overripe fruit.
- Beans, bulbs or seeds from pods.

Plants you can eat

- Papayas, coconuts, bananas, mangoes, sugar cane, cashew nuts, pineapples, palms.
- Young leaves and stems (they taste better).
- Taproots.
- Roots and tubers (they are more nutritious than greens).
- The inner bark of poplars, cottonwoods, willows, birches and conifers, which are good and nutritious
- All grass seeds — they're all edible, but do not eat them if they have turned black.
- Most nuts.

Be careful of berries

Most blue and black berries are edible. Some red berries are edible. Avoid white berries, which are generally poisonous.

🕷 Creepy crawlies

Insects

Don't be squeamish. Insects are castaway gold dust. Plentiful and easy to find and catch, they are also incredibly nutritious, containing up to 80 per cent protein – beef has only 20 per cent. The top delicacies are termites, termite eggs, beetle grubs or larvae, smooth caterpillars, grasshoppers, locusts and crickets (but remove wings and spiny legs first). On a beach, look for sand scarab beetle larvae, which are large fleshy grubs up to 6cm (2.4 inches) long. Don't eat pupae found in the soil. Ants must be cooked for six minutes to destroy formic acid.

To procure a good catch of insects at night, hang some thin material in front of a fire or other light source and place a container of water under it. The insects are attracted to the light, flutter up against the material and drop into the water. Their wings fall off and all you have to do is to the strain the bodies out and roast them over the fire.

Think of how brave Simba the cub was in *The Lion King* and hunt insects early in the morning when they are sluggish. You'll find all manner of juicy bugs in the branches and hollow trunks of trees or under rocks or logs.

Worms

> *Nobody loves me, everybody hates me, I'm gonna go eat worms.*
> *Big fat juicy ones, little tiny squirmy ones, I'm gonna go eat worms.*
> *First you bite the heads off,*
> *Then you squirt the guts out,*
> *Then you throw the skins away.*

The kids' chant 'Nobody loves me' pretty well covers worm eating. Worms are very good bait for catching both fish and birds, and you might consider that a better use for them. However, worms are very rich in protein and they are easy to catch. If you are going to put them on the menu, find the

biggest worms you can, then starve them for a day and then drop them in water, where they will clean themselves. Alternatively, squeeze them hard to excrete the dirt. They can be eaten raw, fried on a hot rock or dried in the sun, ground up and then added as a thickening protein-packed powder to a watery stew. You can be certain of one thing: worms do not taste like chicken.

Slugs and snails

They don't taste like snot. They're much chewier. Snails are packed full of vitamins and minerals and taste much better with garlic and parsley butter. (The butter may be a problem, but wild garlic is often found. If it's around, your nose should lead you to it.) Don't eat snails with brightly coloured shells because nature is telling you to back off, and leave sea snails until they have been identified as edible. Find an enclosed escape-proof space and either leave the slugs and snails to starve themselves clean or feed them herbs and edible greens to clean out any toxins. In the meantime, use them for snail racing competitions. When you are ready to dine, chuck them in salt water to clear out anything that's left. Boil in herb-flavoured water for 10 minutes.

Food checklist

Safe:
- all birds
- non-stinging insects, including ants, grubs and beetles
- worms
- slugs, snails
- all freshwater fish
- shellfish
- seaweed
- most sea fish
- snakes
- lizards
- rodents

Avoid:

- biting or stinging insects (wasps or hornets)
- hairy or brightly coloured insects
- insects feeding on dead bodies or faeces
- spiders, mosquitoes and ticks
- molluscs that are not covered by water at high tide
- brightly coloured frogs
- any animals that you find dead
- fish with poisonous skin
- innards and lungs of crustaceans

Basic tools

Humans are infinitely adaptable, but if you're cast away you may find yourself without tools to cut, dig and hunt with or containers for cooking or food storage. But there is always something you can use.

When animals die, the bones remain and you can make tools from them. You can gouge or hammer with bones, antlers and horns. Deer antlers were used as digging tools by the builders of Stonehenge. The leg of a deer is a source of much bounty: arrows and spearheads from the hoof bones; fishhooks from the foot bones; needles, chisels, awls, hide-working beamers and knives from the long bones. Split and cut the bone to shape with tools or grind between stones. A shoulder blade is the natural shape for a saw: cut out the teeth and sharpen with a file or stone.

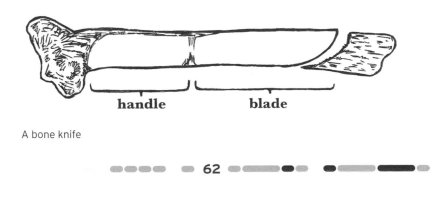

handle   **blade**

A bone knife

The rib bone of any large ruminant (cow, deer, sheep) is ideal for making a bone knife with a 12-cm (4.7-inch) blade. Remove the 'L'-shaped bone at the narrow end of the rib. About 8cm (3 inches) in, split the bone into the marrow cavity from one side only. Cut or file the thick end of the bone into a curve and then sharpen the underside of the blade with a file or a stone until it is sharp enough to cut flesh or hide. To preserve the bone and stop it drying out too much, rub oil or animal fat into it.

As anybody who's cut their hand on a broken bottle can attest, glass is sharp. It's the sharpest material known to mankind. Because it shatters easily, it doesn't make for an effective hunting tool, though shards can be used – very carefully – for gutting and skinning big animals. Obsidian – volcanic glass – can be fractured to produce sharp blades and arrowheads. It is used in cardiac surgery because obsidian blades are five times sharper than surgical-steel scalpels.

Stone can be 'knapped' to make effective tools from flint blades to celts. The celt (pronounced 'selt') is an ungrooved, tapered ground-stone axe made from greenstone, granite or other tough, compact, non-flinty stones. The end of the green wood haft is split, then the tapered rock wedged inside and bound in place using cords.

While flint tools are very sharp, they are brittle, easily damaged and hard to sharpen. To create an edge on stone, you have to hit one stone on to another at less than a right angle. First, bang the top of the rock off as if you were slicing the top off a boiled egg. This creates a flat platform. Then strike down, flaking off shards of stone. A big shard can be sharpened by careful flaking away from the cutting edge with a smaller stone, by polishing, or a combination of the two.

Simple projectile weapons

For hunting birds and small game, a catapult is effective, small, accurate and easy to make. (You can buy wrist catapults from hunting stores that use large ball bearings and are lethal at 50 metres/55 yards).

Find a small, strong branch in the shape of a 'Y'. The prongs should be of equal diameter and the wood needs to be strong and pliable (holly or hazel are excellent). Finding the rubber is the hardest part. Use a cycle inner tube, thick rubber bands or even the elastic from your underpants. Make a little pouch from cloth or leather in the centre of the rubber and tie each end securely to the forked ends of the 'Y'. When hunting birds, load the pouch with several pebbles to increase the chances of hitting your target.

If rubber is scarce and no one will surrender their knickers, make a sling shot using two equal lengths of rope or a leather thong with a small pouch in the middle. Collect a handful of small round pebbles 2cm (0.8 inch) in diameter. Place one in the centre of the pouch and then swing the sling around your head in a circle. When you think you are lined up with your target let one end go. While it worked for David against Goliath, using a sling needs practice. This should be done well away from other people.

Containers

All sorts of bark can be used to make containers, but birch bark is the best. Native Americans who lived close to the northern forests used it for everything from tepee coverings to canoes to cooking containers. When they were first introduced to metal cooking pots, the women were unimpressed. They were heavy and wouldn't fold up when the camp was on the move.

Birch bark contains natural waxes that make it waterproof and resistant to rot, but also highly flammable. It is excellent wet-weather kindling, and loose rolls of thin bark make an effective torch. Wind it tight in a string and you have a candle. You can also make a container from birch bark in minutes.

To make a container that can hold hot grease, cut a rectangular piece of bark. Make a series of light scratches where you are going to fold. To make sharp folds at the corners without cracking the bark, heat it gently along the fold. Make the fold before the bark cools and make sure the edges match perfectly. Fold in the first corner and repeat the process. The box can be secured either by stitching or using wooden pegs (see below).

Basic containers can also be hollowed out of wood. Take a dry log or tree root (they are easier to burn out) of the right diameter and cut off a length. Place the ends of two or more sticks in the fire and burn the tips into hot coals. Apply the hot coals to the surface of the container you are making so that the surface burns and turns into charcoal. Scrape out the charcoal if it gets too hot. It will take an hour or so to burn a decent-sized container, though you can speed it up by blowing through a straw. Don't burn the edges too thin. When it is deep enough, chuck water on and chop out the rest of the charcoal. Scrape it clean with a knife and polish it with sand.

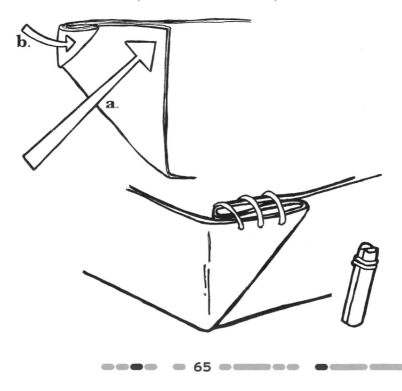

Get knotted

Almost everything you make will have to be tied together. There are dozens of different knots and almost as many variations on each one. Watching an expert tie knots is akin to seeing a concert pianist, demonstrating that the quickness of the hand deceives the eye. The skill you are admiring comes from years of practice. Most people know how to tie only a reef knot and half the time that ends up a granny that doesn't work properly.

If a member of the group knows their knots, ask them to teach you these six. Then practise tying them again and again until you can do them blindfolded.

Reef knot

This was originally used on sailing ships to reef sails. It is simple to tie and easy to undo. It is not effective on ropes of different thicknesses or for nylon, but is practical in first aid, since it lies flat against the skin. Golden rule: left over right, right over left.

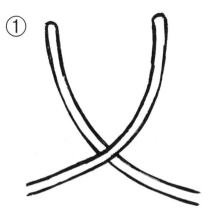

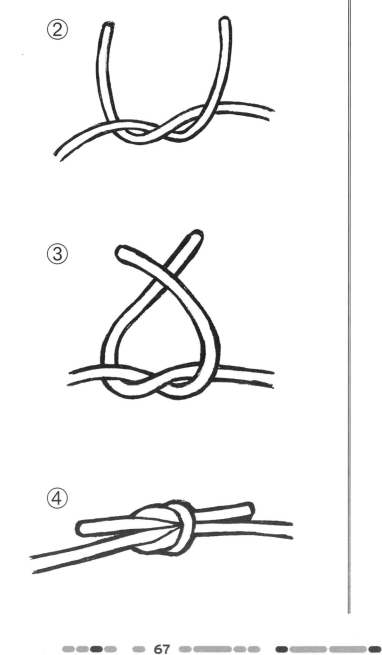

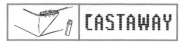

Clove hitch

This is a quick-fix knot for attaching ropes to a post, for example tying up a boat or a horse.

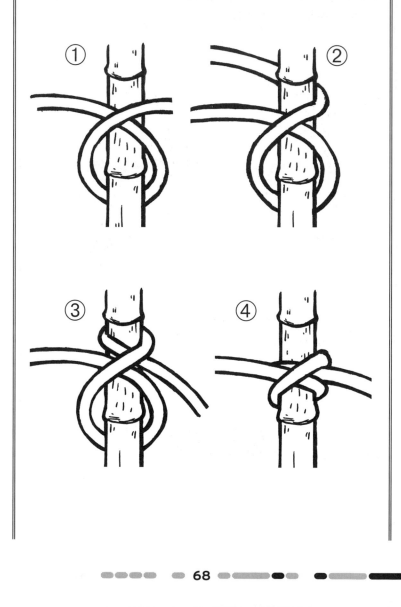

Figure eight

This is a stopper, used at the end of a rope to prevent it slipping through a hole. A double figure of eight with a loop at the end can be hooked over the end of a spike. The double eight gives extra weight, which makes it easier to throw.

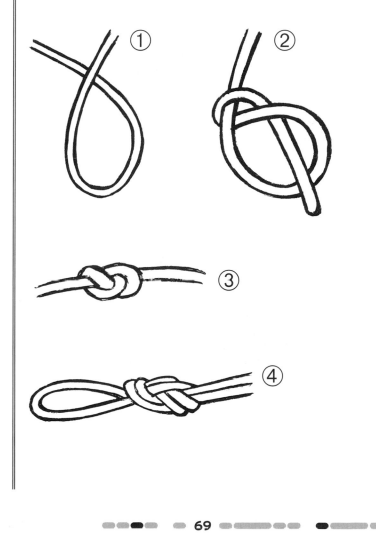

Sheet bend

An excellent way of fastening two differently sized ropes so they don't slip.

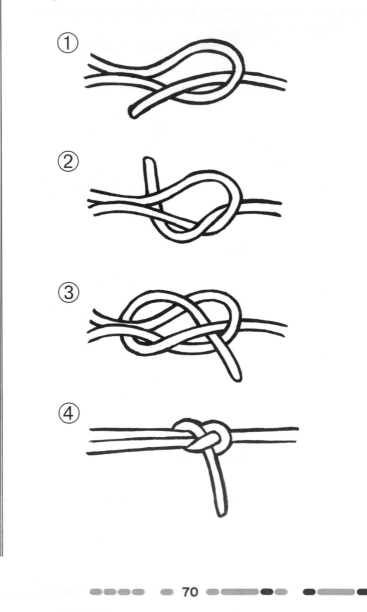

Bowline

Almost as useful as the reef knot to create a fixed loop that will not tighten or slip under strain. It does take a lot of practice. Think of the loop as the rabbit hole; the tip as the rabbit; the other end (the long end) of the rope as the tree.

- **Make a loop. Feed the rabbit tip up through the hole.**
- **Pass the rabbit around the back of the tree (under the rope).**
- **Bring rabbit tip back up and down the hole again. Pull tight.**

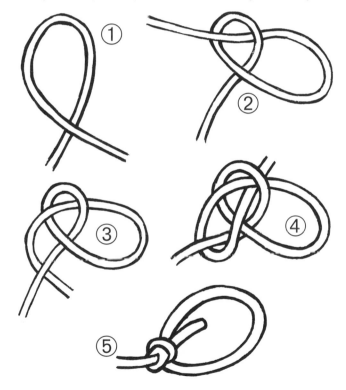

You can make a simple lasso or running bowline by passing the other end of the rope through your bowline loop. Never tie a running bowline around your waist: if it gets tightened accidentally it could kill.

Fisherman's knot

Excellent for tying together two thin, slippery lines – fishing line, wires, vines. It is hard to untie and does not work that well on nylon rope.

- Lay lines down together, tips facing in opposite directions.
- Take the tip of one end over the other and make an overhand loop (make a loop and pass the tip back through it).
- Do same with the other tip.
- Partially tighten each knot and slide towards each other. Once the knots rest together they should be fully tight.

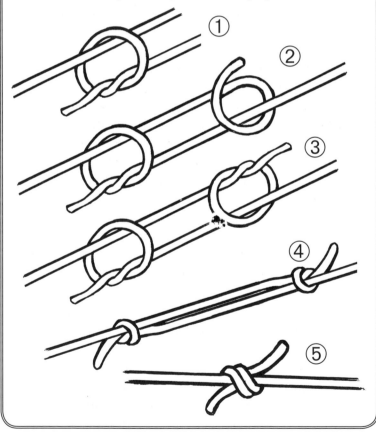

Castaway cooking for beginners

Unless you have absolutely no means of lighting a fire, you must cook your food. There's no time to faff about with different fancy cuts and *grande cuisine*. Basic cooking is simply a compromise between destroying the nutrients of the food you have collected and improving its taste and digestibility. Cooking will also kill some poisonous and disease-carrying substances. If you cook food too much, it will remove the vitamins, minerals and calories and you needn't have bothered.

How to cook using a campfire

Simple, innit? Take lump of meat, or large fish, shove a sharpened stick through it, hold stick over flames, enjoy the exquisite flavours of freshly flame-grilled food.

While this might work with marshmallows it is the perfect recipe for going hungry or getting sick. Your stick may burn through, dropping your supper into the fire, where it will be frazzled into a lump of blackened shoe leather. The heat may cause the meat to disintegrate and fall into the fire. Assuming none of these things happen, you will still end up with piece of blackened meat that burns your mouth yet is cold and raw in the middle. If there are any nasties lurking inside they will remain unscathed and eager to invade a new host.

Campfire cooking is best done over hot ashes and embers, where the cooking process can be monitored and controlled. There should be more than enough heat. It is easier to cook over a parallel fire (longer than it is wide) – or dig a narrow trench and build the fire in that.

While the flames are still high, start boiling water (unless your supplies are low). Do not underestimate the value of having hot water to hand. It can be used to sterilise wounds and provide warming drinks.

To boil water you need a metal cooking pot, preferably with a wire handle (for boiling water *without* a pot, see 'Boiling food', page 76). This can then be suspended above the flames using a rope or a hooked stick.

The simplest suspension device is a three-legged tripod. Pick three branches of roughly equal length and thickness. The legs should be long enough so that their bases won't be too near the fire. Sharpen the ends of the legs so they can be driven into the ground to create a strong base, lash them together and hang the pot over the flames.

There are other variations. Place a small tripod about 30cm (1 foot) away from the fire. Lay a long branch across it. Anchor one end with rocks or legs, then hang the cooking pot from the other end. When building a trench fire to cook, make sure the edges of the trench are narrower than the cooking pot. Put green logs underneath the pot for added support. In another variation you can lash one end of a strong pole to a standing tree and support the pole with two sticks lashed together. (A fire should always be at least 2 metres (2.2 yards) away from a living tree.)

The high-bar suspension is pretty much what it sounds like – a horizontal bar at head height over a parallel fire. With this you can cook with more than one pot. The poles at the ends are driven deep enough into the ground to be able to take the weight of the bar and are positioned half a step away from the fire to remain safe. The tops of the posts are tied to the horizontal bar for added security.

The same basic construction can be used to spit-roast meat. If you are roasting over an open fire, the spit should be slightly off to one side with a metal tray or clean bark receptacle underneath to catch the fat, which should be used for basting. If you are cooking on embers, the spit can be directly over the fire.

Your choices of cooking methods in the bush are basic. Boil it. Or broil it.

Broiling is when you expose food directly to the fire or its coals. The thinner the cut of meat, the easier it is to cook it properly. For bigger animals such as rabbit and squirrel, cut along the backbone so it resembles a

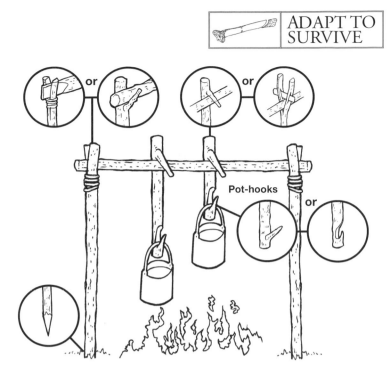

Horizontal bar cooking

spatchcocked chicken. Fish can be prepared in the same way. Gutting by cutting down the backbone (not the belly) makes it easier to cook the flesh evenly. Do not remove the scales from fish. They will char as the flesh cooks through the skin, and can act as a handy all-in-one pan and plate.

Planking is a similar utensil-free way to cook fish and thin slices of meat. Cut a log in half and make the surface as flat as possible. Peg the meat on to the flat side and push the log close enough to the fire so that food cooks. If you have a thicker cut, unpeg and turn it over. Or use a thin slab of rock as your pan. Before building the fire find a rock about 2.5cm (1 inch) thick. Arrange two or three other rocks as a base, build a fire between them and when it's hot enough place your slab pan on top of the base. Alternatively, you can cook using a vertical rock slab. Simply tilt the rock up by the fire and let it heat all the way through. Once it is hot enough, the meat or fish will stick to the rock. One side will be cooked by the rock, the other by the fire.

Grilling food wastes essential fat, so should be employed only when you have good supplies.

Boiling food

Boiling is the easiest and safest way of cooking in the wild. It bursts the fibres and cells of meat and vegetables, making them easier to eat and digest – though the bland taste often leaves much to be desired. Boiling loses fewer of the nutrients and less of the fat, and the cooking water can be used for stews and soups. Boiling meat, especially aquatic animals, for half an hour should kill off any nasties. If you want to restore a bit of flavour you can always broil the meat afterwards.

But how do you boil water if you don't have a metal saucepan? Native Americans managed very well by dropping red-hot stones the size of eggs into water containers made of bark or hollowed-out wood. In tropical conditions, you can use empty coconut shells, although they are a bit small. Bamboo is better. Fill a tube of thick bamboo with water and then, supporting it with a forked stick, angle it across the fire. Be careful not to let any natural container boil dry or it will crack and burn.

Rock on

Hot rocks can be used to cook birds and fish from the inside out. Find a rock that fits inside the body cavity. Heat it until red-hot, place it inside your meal and bind in place. Pack the bird or fish in insulation such as dried grass or old man's beard. Leave for four hours or until the rock has cooled.

A thorny digression – cooking in clay

In medieval times people believed that eating hedgehogs could cure a wide variety of ailments, including leprosy, colic, boils, kidney stones and poor vision. Back in the fourteenth century Konrad of Megenberg wrote that:

> '...the flesh of the hedgehog is wholesome for the stomach and strengthens the same. Likewise it hath a power of drying and relieving the stomach. It deals with the water of dropsy and is of great help to such as are inclined to the sickness called elephantiasis.'

Some Europeans believe eating hedgehogs is a cure for poisoning and removes curses.

Unfortunate as this is for Mrs Tiggywinkle, she does possess a formidable and spiky armour. The best way to cook a hedgehog – and indeed a porcupine – is to roll them in clay, then chuck the clay ball in the fire. When the clay is rock-hard, fish it out, break open and peel back the baked clay, which takes the spines with it.

The principle is equally effective for small game and birds. It has the advantage of cutting down prep time and obviates the need for cooking utensils and washing up. Animals and reptiles must be cleaned and gutted, while big birds should be plucked, but otherwise fur, scales and feathers all conveniently come off with the clay.

SHIT HAPPENS!: Wild animals

Wild animals do their best to avoid confrontations with humans, because we're unpredictable, violent and have questionable dress sense – and there are a lot of us. Likewise, we should aim to avoid them, because, when an animal believes it is cornered, it can get even more dangerous.

Bears are not cuddly. Polar bears can remove your head with one casual swipe. Bears, while not naturally man eaters, are scavengers, which means they will come to campsites in search of food. Store food so that it cannot be smelled, and dig a rubbish pit. The easiest way to drive away a bear – or other scavengers such as hyenas – is to make a loud noise. Do not climb a tree, since most bears are probably better at climbing than you. If that fails and the bear still attacks, strike back, going for the eyes or snout. Make yourself as big as possible and shout as loudly as you can. A prayer might help.

If confronted by cougars, lions or other big cats, do not run away. This makes you look like prey. Your survival depends on convincing this big cat that you might be dangerous. Make yourself bigger by opening your coat wide, hold your ground, wave your arms, and shout. Show it that you are not defenceless by throwing stones while backing slowly away. If you have a fire, try to get an ember. If it does attack, hit it on the head aiming for the eyes and nose.

Wild pigs have sharp tusks and a vicious bite. They may charge you if you're in their territory and they can sever the femoral artery. If this happens stop the bleeding fast – see page 210.

Unlike most wild animals, crocodiles and alligators are not scared of humans. During World War Two, British troops had encircled a

thousand Japanese soldiers. The Japanese soldiers tried to escape
at night through a mangrove swamp on Ramree Island off the Burma
coast. Between British gunfire and saltwater crocodiles, only about
twenty Japanese survived.

Crocs and gators are found near swamps, rivers and tidal pools. Never
enter the water at dusk and stay well clear of their nests and eggs.
Should you meet one, back slowly away, watching out for the tail,
which moves fast like a scythe. If it comes towards you, try to hit it
on the nose or in the eyes with a stick. If it bites you, punch its snout
hard to make it open its mouth. Holding a bandana over its eyes may
calm it down. And they can't climb trees.

4

WHERE AM I?

CASTAWAY

'I was wet, had not clothes to shift me, nor any thing either to eat or drink to comfort me, neither did I see any prospect before me, but that of perishing with hunger, or being devour'd by wild beasts ... this threw me into terrible agonies of mind, that for a while I run about like a mad-man.'

Daniel Defoe, *Robinson Crusoe*

Although Daniel Defoe had never been anywhere near a desert island, *Robinson Crusoe* is a great role model for today's castaway. His fears and the way he deals with them are almost identical to those of a modern castaway, and he displays many of the qualities that experts today tell you determine why some individuals make it and some don't.

When Crusoe first realises he is shipwrecked, he goes into a panic. Deep fears about being consumed by 'ravenous beasts' cause him to sleep in a tree on his first night. Nevertheless, he gets a good rest, and the next day is kept busy salvaging what he can from the wreck of the ship. There are even moments of euphoria as he finds food, gunpowder and a carpenter's chest – 'much more valuable than a ship loading of gold would have been at that time'.

That night the fears return, and he builds a substantial barricade around his sailcloth tent. Later, he admits that there was never any real risk of attack from man or beast, but that he was simply terrified by his new situation.

He soon discovers that the island has fresh water and an 'abundance of fowls' and within a couple of days he decides that the first location he chose for his tent is wrong. On low, swampy ground, the site is not 'wholesome', and is also distant from fresh water. He sets about finding somewhere near fresh water, with shelter from the heat of the sun and safety from wild animals. The best spot is inland, but he determines that he must have a view over the sea 'that if God sent any ship in sight, I might not lose any advantage for my deliverance'.

He then spends a year constructing his new home, which includes a cave
that Crusoe gradually expands. In his 'fancy' he calls it his 'kitchen', and
lovingly equips it with shelves. The building work is part of a rigid routine,
involving hunting, working, sleep, and 'time of diversion'. He makes a
calendar by digging notches on a stick to be able to mark the Sabbath.
Although not, at this point, a religious man, Crusoe fears losing the routine
of observing a day of rest, something that gave shape to his old life.

Further crises of confidence do follow, but Crusoe survives through keeping
busy and thinking positively. 'I had a dismal prospect of my condition,' he
says. 'Tears would run plentifully down my face ... But something always
return'd swift upon me to check these thoughts.' He consoles himself that
he alone of those onboard was not drowned, and how lucky he was that
a helpful storm washed the ship and its vital provisions within reach of
the beach. Every negative thought or experience spurs him to count his
blessings. After he nearly perishes when his homemade raft is swept out to
sea, he appreciates anew the dry land of his island. 'Thus we never ... know
how to value what we enjoy but by the want of it.'

Having never handled a tool in his life, he finds it a slow learning process,
requiring huge patience. Building a spade out of a particularly hard piece of
wood takes weeks. Then he moves on to a chair and table, which also take ages,
but each achievement gives him pride and renews his determination to survive.

'Time and necessity,' he writes, 'made me a compleat natural mechanick.'
Thus, he says, 'I had learn'd not to despair of any thing.'

CASTAWAY

Mental qualities for survival

The most important mental qualities for a castaway's survival include:

- an ability to improvise;
- an ability to hope for the best, but plan for the worst;
- an abundance of patience;
- an ability to make up your mind;
- an ability to simply take it;
- a sense of humour;
- an ability to set goals; and
- an ability to keep cool, calm and collected.

Those who survive manage, somehow, to retain an inner sanctum of calm, whatever the circumstances. Courage, inner strength, resourcefulness, initiative and innovation are just as important as basic survival skills. Of these, inner strength – the will to live – is the most important.

Crusoe, for all his positive thinking and busy ingenuity, still refers to his island as his prison. He feels the lack of human company deeply, and adopts various animals as companions. The effects of solitary confinement are grim. Being deprived of social interaction can lead to perceptual distortions, illusions, vivid fantasies (sometimes along with vivid hallucinations) and hyperresponsivity to external stimuli. It can even cause organic changes in the brain similar to stupor and delirium. In 1956, Dr Milton Meltzer, former chief medical officer at Alcatraz Prison, wrote about prisoners who were punished in solitary confinement. As well as noting loss of motor skills, he observed that the 'sense of self, the ego and the ego boundary phenomena are profoundly affected by the isolation'. So important are other people to our sense of self that their absence leads the solitary castaway to doubt himself and have trouble determining what is real – what psychiatrists call *overt psychotic disorganisation*. Crusoe solves some of his identity crisis and need to communicate by writing every day and creating an imaginary friend. In the film *Cast Away* (2000), Chuck Noland (Tom Hanks) talks to a basketball with a face painted on. For Robinson Crusoe, it was God. He starts praying for the first time in his life.

🦟 Challenges

Whether alone or in a group, once landed into any new environment, each individual faces particular challenges. Some of the challenges are purely physical. Because your body is exposed to new and unfamiliar environmental conditions and unfamiliar germs, you may be prone to intestinal upsets, colds or flu. To adjust as quickly as possible, force yourself to get up, stay active during the day and expose yourself to lots of sunlight, as this helps reset the body's internal clock.

For the first few days, rest and recuperation are vital, as exhaustion can sap your morale, make you more prone to illness, less effective at the tasks you need to do and more irritable about having to face the constant challenges of daily life.

States of adjustment

Most people, when confronted by challenging or dislocating experiences, go through distinct phases. First is the 'honeymoon period', a time of excitement and adrenalin rush. Make the most of it: explore your new surroundings, make friends in the group, gain experience and confidence in your competence. People in groups who share this honeymoon period can develop strong and lasting bonds.

The more 'plugged in' you can get during this phase, the better you will ride out the 'slump' that might lie ahead. Until this point, you draw on a psychological reserve tank stocked with security, self-confidence and energy from your previous existence. Eventually, you will exhaust these reserves, and may find yourself sinking into the 'slump' or 'transition shock'. Some, overwhelmed by the whole experience, can miss out the honeymoon period and immediately slide into depression. Typical symptoms include feelings of being overpowered, homesickness, a drop in self-confidence, mild depression, irritability and hostility.

Human beings make sense of the world and their lives by following routines and taking familiar things for granted. But nothing is obvious any more;

everything takes work to figure out, and much more to actually accomplish. With everything changed, you may feel assaulted or bewildered by the physical environment and your new circumstances.

To help cope with this, consciously put structure and predictability into your life by establishing daily routines for meals, work and leisure time. Learning about your new environment will help you feel more comfortable and confident, but don't overwhelm yourself by trying to learn everything at once.

For a castaway, homesickness is more than missing friends, family, familiar places and activities. There is the possibility that you will never return to your old life. Grief for these losses is natural and real, and you must face and work through it.

What happened to your self-confidence?

Being dislocated from your normal environment can be a heavy blow to the ego. You may find yourself unable to perform tasks that you previously took for granted and may be dependent on someone like never before.

To overcome this, work on becoming an 'expert' on some aspect of your new environment, be it food, fuel, shelter or even the latrine. Help others because by doing that you become a rescuer, not a victim. Seeing how your leadership and skills buoy others up gives you more focus and energy to persevere.

Find ways to remain 'true to yourself'. Get creative about following the inclinations that help define your sense of self. Decorating your shack may not seem as pressing as searching for food, but the psychological nourishment it provides might be even more important – and an example to others.

Temporary depression

Signs of depression are insomnia or excessive sleeping, not eating or overindulging, bouts of crying and excessive self-criticism. To counter this, keep busy – make sure you are scheduled to do something the next day. Try not to bottle up your negative feelings. Express them to your companions, or write them down. Most of all, admit them to yourself, and acknowledge them as normal.

Hostility and irritation

Snapping at a companion or crying over a trivial issue is all part of the adjustment process. When you feel like bitching or pounding something or somebody out of sheer frustration, practise stress-reducing techniques that work for you. Tensing and then relaxing your muscles is very effective, and so are yoga, meditation and even taking a long walk. If you find yourself feeling angry, work out what is bothering you most. Asking your companions for help, rather than blaming them, is a more effective route to a solution.

Most important of all, keep your sense of humour, even in extreme adversity. Laugh at threats. When people are fighting for their lives, laughter makes them more calm, helping their chance of survival.

Personal hygiene

The battle for survival is won in the head. Special-forces soldiers place great importance on washing and shaving every day, of keeping their hair short and groomed. It shows that they are stronger than the environment in which they are temporarily stranded. It's important – no, vital – to keep up appearances. Unless you are stuck in the snow at way below zero, where taking off your clothes is an altogether stupid idea, smelling bad sends out the wrong message to your companions and yourself. It says you don't care. Personal hygiene is of paramount importance. Cleanliness helps prevent infection and disease. You can keep clean without a power shower and scented soap from Paris. Washing with soap is not so important. It makes the skin less waterproof and more prone to infection.

During the Crimean War, Florence Nightingale announced that a pint of water a day was enough to keep clean. Using a clean cloth, you can sponge your face, armpits, crotch and feet every day.

You don't need soap. Try rubbing dry sand or ash all over your body. The abrasive material will remove the dirt along with layers of dead skin. People pay hundreds of pounds for such exfoliation treatments. To reduce lice infestation on the body or hair make a nettle body wash and shampoo. Mix the juice of crushed nettles 50/50 with water. Rub it all over. No, it won't sting. In the desert where water is scarce, nomads wash their hair with urine, which is antiseptic, and scrape their skin with oil.

There's always the 'air bath'. Remove as much of your clothing as is practical and expose your body to the sun and air for at least one hour. The sun is very effective at zapping diseases, as few bacteria or viruses can survive long exposure to ultraviolet light. Be careful not to burn.

While you may not need soap to keep your body clean you will need it to sterilise your hands before administering first aid and to clean wounds. It's also useful for washing clothes, especially if you are living by the sea, where salt encrustation will destroy them fast.

Making soap

Soap is made from oil and alkali. All you need to make your very own is animal fat, a cooking pot, a fire and an old sock. Something that doubles as a shallow dish is helpful but not essential.

First, cut the fat into small pieces and cook them in a pot with enough water to keep the fat from sticking as it cooks. Cook slowly, stirring frequently. Once the fat is rendered, drain off the grease into a container to harden.

Take your clean sock and fill it with cold crushed ash from the fire. Soak the sock in water and hang it up so that the water and ash drip out. This is potash or lye. If you don't have a sock, use a long sleeve, but don't forget to knot the end.

In the cooking pot, mix two parts grease to one part lye. To make antiseptic soap add pine needles or horseradish root. Boil the mixture until it thickens to the consistency of porridge, then allow to cool.

After the mixture – the soap – cools, you can use it in this semiliquid state or pour it into a flat container; allow it to harden before cutting it into bars for later use. Store in a cool dry place unless you want puddles of liquid soap.

Looking after your body

Hands
Take special care to keep your hands clean. Germs on your hands can infect food and wounds. Wash them after handling anything likely to carry germs, after visiting the latrine and caring for the sick, and before touching any food, food utensils or drinking water. Keep your fingernails closely trimmed and clean, and your fingers out of your mouth.

Hair
The hair on your head, your armpits and pubic hair can become a haven for bacteria or fleas, lice, and other parasites. Keeping hair cut short and occasionally rinsed with cold water should suffice. (Do not throw cut hair away: it makes great tinder.) Combing frequently will remove lice.

Clothes

Keeping clothing and bedding as clean as possible will reduce the chance of skin infection and the danger of parasitic infestation. If possible, clean your clothing whenever it becomes soiled and change your underwear and socks daily. Try to shake, air and sun your dirty clothes for two hours every day. Turn sleeping bags inside out to air every day.

Teeth

Thoroughly clean your mouth and teeth at least once each day. If you don't have a toothbrush, make a chewing stick. Find a twig about 20cm (8 inches) long and 1cm (0.5 inch) wide. Chew one end to separate the fibres and brush your teeth thoroughly. Or wrap a clean strip of cloth around your fingers and rub your teeth to wipe away food particles. You can brush your teeth with small amounts of sand, salt or soap, then rinse your mouth with water, salt water or bark or herb tea. Flossing can be done with strips of nylon fishing line or plant fibre.

If you have toothache, chew cloves: they act as an anaesthetic. Cavities can be temporarily filled with candle wax. Make sure you clean the cavity by rinsing with salt water or picking any particles out before pouring in the wax.

Feet

You need them, especially if you are undertaking a long escape march. Inspect daily to make sure they are dry and free of infection. If you can walk around barefoot without lacerating your soles or picking up tropical nasties, try to do so, thus hardening your feet as well as reducing wear on shoes and boots. Keep your toenails trimmed flat – do not rip them off.

Ingrown toenails need to be treated as soon as they develop. Removing the nail is a bad idea, since the toe will then need to be dressed and you may not be able to walk. Take the razorblade from your survival kit and put a small piece of plastic underneath the top of the nail to avoid cutting the toe. Gently shave the middle third of the nail from the cuticle to the tip. Once the nail is thin enough it will buckle into a ridge, relieving the pressure.

❧ Exploration

If you are on an island, you will want to establish as soon as possible whether it is inhabited. In any event, you will want to explore your environment to 'plug in' to your new surroundings.

Even the most obvious rules are often ignored. Always explore in groups of at least two people. Remember your trail by taking mental notes of landmarks, or by making physical marks along the route. Before setting out, tell others what form the marks will take. Make sure you have sufficient provisions and footwear. Don't attempt anything remotely resembling mountaineering unless you are properly trained and equipped. It is usually safer to go around such obstacles. Always carry a walking stick. You can use it to test the ground, help you cross water and support your weight.

If you smell smoke or see animals acting nervously, check for fire. If the wind is blowing towards the fire, move into the wind. Look for a stream or a clearing in the trees where there would be little fuel for the fire. Lie down, breathe close to the ground and stay there until the fire has passed. If you can, wet your clothing and put a jacket over your head. Cover your mouth with a handkerchief so that you don't breathe in too much smoke.

Don't underestimate the dangers of water. If it is very cold, it can shock you into taking a sharp breath, which if you are submerged means lungfuls of choking water. Slow-moving rivers can still have a powerful current, and the water can hide dangerous obstacles. Assess the current by throwing a stick into the water. Never cross a stream in the dark, or if the other side is not visible. To ford a river, look for a straight section where the river bed is firm and the water shallow. Keep your shoes on and cross slowly, using a walking stick for support.

While a compass is the single most important piece of kit for exploration, there are ways to get by without one. In the northern hemisphere, when the sun is at its highest point of the day, it is due south. In the southern hemisphere it is due north. An easier way to determine compass points is to

put a three-foot stick upright on level ground and make a mark with a stone where the tip of the shadow falls. Fifteen minutes later, make a new mark where the tip of the shadow now falls. The line between these two points is east-west, with the first marker on the western side. North and south, of course, lie on a line bisecting this at right angles.

If you have a piece of iron wire, a razorblade or a needle, it is possible to make a compass yourself. Magnetise the metal by rubbing it on clothing in one direction only or gently heating it, and then suspend it from its middle on a thread. It will point north.

Maps are vital for finding your way back to camp and for marking resources so that you can find them again. Make a map by plotting landmarks, oddly shaped stones, large trees or watercourses. Start by getting the best possible vantage point – at the top of a hill or just by climbing a tree – and marking ridges of high ground. This shows you where the valleys are, which might contain rivers or streams. Fill in the details of your map as your exploration continues.

Keep a lookout at all times for new food, water or fuel sources. Like Crusoe, keep looking for a more 'wholesome' permanent campsite. Observe what happens to various areas when the weather, wind or tide changes. Check out the usual wind direction by looking at how nearby plants are growing or observing drift marks on sand dunes and snow.

As you explore you will gain a picture of your new home, of the nature that surrounds it and of the weather patterns that affect it. Before you settle on a new location you need to know what weather it will have to protect you from.

But how do you know what is around the corner?

Weather

The Boxing Day Tsunami of 2004 killed more than 230,000 people in a dozen countries surrounding the Bay of Bengal. Yet five Stone Age tribes in the remote Andaman and Nicobar Islands escaped unscathed because they fled to the forests and higher ground before the tsunami hit. When the sea dramatically receded prior to the tidal waves hitting the shore, 'civilised' people ran down to see what was happening, but the Shompen legged it inland. How did they know what to do?

It might be as simple as the natural human flight reaction working at full throttle without the brain asking why and getting in the way. More likely, it was that they and the other tribes who live in the archipelago – the Onges, Jarawas, Sentinalese and Great Andamanese – had read nature's early-warning system and understood it.

Those tribes number only a few hundred each, but they live, as they have done for thousands of years, close to nature. They know to heed biological warning signs such as changes in the cries of birds and the behaviour patterns of land and marine animals. The tribal leaders say that the earth communicates to them and they can 'smell the wind, gauge the depth of the sea with the sound of their oars', according to Ashish Roy, an environmentalist and lawyer from the region. When the jungle dwellers saw the animals run for high ground they followed suit.

Generations of observation and passing on that knowledge saved their lives. No wonder they fired arrows at the search helicopters. They didn't need rescue.

Watching the weather

Living in a city in Western Europe, you are in an environment that has been designed to be immune from nature. A castaway, in contrast, has no heating, no air conditioning and no shelter from the rain. As every true Brit knows, islands have more unpredictable and fast-changing weather than continents. Understanding and adapting to weather patterns is essential to your survival.

Look at the animals

Most animals are vulnerable to environmental changes that humans often can't detect. Swallows flying low may indicate the air pressure is dropping. Falling pressure affects the digestive system of ruminants such as cows, making them less willing to go to pasture, causing them to lie down. The calls of some birds, including crows and geese, become more frequent with falling pressure.

If a storm is coming, squirrels sense the bad weather and strip the tree of acorns. Deer and elk react to wind and air pressure by coming down from mountains and seeking shelter. Rabbits, rattlesnakes and certain fish feed more before a storm.

Cicadas can't vibrate their wings when the humidity is very high, so may be silent when rain is approaching. Flying insects are more active when the air pressure drops and stay closer to the ground, so before a rain storm they seem to be swarming. The birds that eat them, therefore, feed lower before bad weather arrives.

Some flowers close up as the humidity rises, so rain doesn't wash away their pollen. The leaves of some trees curl up, while pine cones close their scales just before a storm.

We're animals, too, so our bodies sense changing weather. Senses increase. The smell of vegetation heightens before rain. The higher the humidity, the better sound travels. English country folk gauged the chances of rain by the clarity with which they heard the church bells.

Don't forget the old adage, 'When your joints hurt, a storm is coming'. Low air pressure and dampness cause aching in arthritic joints, bad teeth, recently healed broken bones and corns and bunions. Curly hair becomes tighter and even more unmanageable while straight hair goes straighter still.

If the smoke from your fire is rising straight up, the weather will remain fine; if the smoke is swirling about or beaten down by an invisible hand, prepare for rain.

Old clichés, real weather

There's a reason for all those old sayings about the weather – thousands of years of observation – but they are not all set in stone.

'Red sky at night, shepherds' delight' (some prefer the more poetic 'The sky is red, the devil is dead, it's going to be good tomorrow') or the opposite, 'Red sky in the morning, shepherds' warning', both have a solid basis in science. Weather systems typically move from west to east, and red clouds result when the sun shines on their undersides at either sunrise or sunset. If the morning skies are red, it is likely that clear skies to the east permit the sun to light the undersides of moisture-bearing clouds coming in from the west. In the tropics (5–20 degrees latitude) weather systems move from east to west, so the opposite would apply. A grey morning suggests a dry day, while a grey evening tells you that rain is on its way.

Cloud watching

Studying clouds will give an indication of what is going on. There are only three types of cloud – cirrus, cumulus and stratus. These three names, alone and combined with other Latin words such as nimbus, are used to identify different cloud formations.

Cirrus are the very high (6km/3.7 miles or more) clouds that look like thin streaks or curls, sometimes referred to as horses' tails. They are usually a sign of fair weather, although in cold climates cirrus clouds that begin to multiply and are accompanied by increasing winds blowing steadily from the north indicate an oncoming blizzard.

Cumulus are the fluffy, white, heaped-up, cotton-wool clouds. Much lower than cirrus clouds, they are generally fair-weather clouds appearing around midday on a sunny day. As the day advances, they may become bigger and push higher into the atmosphere, piling up into cloud mountains and towers. These can turn into storm clouds.

Stratus clouds are very low, grey clouds, often covering the whole sky in an even grey layer. They generally mean rain.

Cloud variations

- Nimbus clouds are rain clouds of uniform greyness that extend over the entire sky.
- Nimbostratus is a heavy, dark layer covering the sky. Get under cover: it's going to pour.
- Cumulonimbus is the cloud formation resulting from a cumulus cloud building up, extending to great heights, and forming the shape of an anvil (known as cumulonimbus incus or thunderhead). Expect a thunderstorm if it's heading in your direction.
- Cirrostratus is a fairly uniform layer of high-stratus clouds that are darker than cirrus clouds.
- Cirrocumulus is a small, white, round cloud at a high altitude. Both this and cirrostratus indicate good weather.
- Scuds do not bode well. They are loose, vapour-like clouds driven before the wind and a sign of continuing bad weather.

Cloud study: The 'crossed-winds' rule

By standing with your back to the ground-level wind and observing the movement of the clouds, it is possible to determine whether the weather will improve or deteriorate. In the northern hemisphere, if the upper-level clouds are moving from the right, a low-pressure area has passed and the weather will improve; if they are moving from the left, a low-pressure area is arriving and the weather will deteriorate (reverse for the southern hemisphere). Clouds travelling parallel to but against the wind may indicate a thunderstorm approaching. Outflow winds typically blow opposite to the updraft zone, and clouds carried in the upper-level wind will appear to be moving against the surface wind.

The unmistakable herringbone pattern of a mackerel sky and the long, wispy cirrus are all high-altitude indicators that a rainy low-pressure system is moving in from the west. This usually means an increase in wind speeds, a shift to blustery easterly winds and increased cloud and rain within the next 24 hours.

Howling at the moon

A halo or corona around the sun or moon is caused by the refraction of that body's light by ice crystals at high altitude. This shows that moisture is moving in at increasingly lower levels, and indicates that an active weather system is on its way.

The effect of the moon on weather is indirect in that it affects ocean tides, which in turn can alter ocean currents that can affect weather. The greatest tidal variations are at the new and full moons. Statistically, 10 per cent more rain and the heaviest downpours occur in the days following new or full moons. That's when ski resorts expect the most snow and tropical storms can become hurricanes.

Forecasting

If you would like your own homemade meteorologist, cut a weather stick from fir, willow or birch, generally about 40cm (15–16 inches) long and the thickness of a switch. Mount it outside on the horizontal. It will twist upwards with the onset of good weather and downwards as bad weather approaches. Balsam fir sticks were first used by Native Americans in the US northeast and eastern Canada. They noted the behaviour of dry branches prior to the arrival of weather changes.

If you want to know how hot it is, count the number of cricket chirps in a fourteen-second period and add forty. For 75 per cent of the time, the total will equal the current air temperature to within one degree Fahrenheit.

SHIT HAPPENS! Things that bite in the night – and the day

Lucy Irvine lived with Gerald Kingsland on Tuin island off the northernmost coast of Australia from May 1981 to June 1982. As she wrote in her bestselling book, *Castaway*, they suffered a severe shortage of food and water, and were beset with illnesses and dangers, including shark attack and dangerous wildlife. They shared their hut with more than forty poisonous spiders, but they didn't bother them. In fact, it was a series of tiny bites and cuts on their legs from sandflies and toxic coral that almost brought an early end to their adventure. Gerald's wounds became so infected he could not walk.

Sandflies are attracted to moisture as well as food or waste left out. They can cause infection – known as sandfly fever – if they get

at an open wound. The symptoms are headaches and bloodshot eyes. They may or may not be deterred by insect repellent, so it is better to sleep off the ground, or move to a more breezy spot.

Centipedes and millipedes are usually harmless, although some can grow as large as 25cm (10 inches). Their legs can dig in to your flesh, causing a risk of infection, or they can give you a sharp bite. If you see one on you, brush it off in the direction it is travelling. They have been known to curl up in the most intimate places of a sleeping person, giving you a nasty shock when you wake up.

Typically between 1.2 and 5cm (0.6–2 inches) long and usually black, brown or sometimes spotted with bright colours, **assassin bugs** feed on blood or other insects. They are also called 'kissing bugs' from their ability to steal a meal by piercing the lips, eyelids or ears of a sleeping human. Assassin bugs have a flat, narrow body with an abdomen that is sometimes widened in the middle. Its long narrow head holds the deadly weapon it uses to prey on its victims – a segmented proboscis. They can hide out in bathtubs, sinks and drains, but they are more commonly found in savanna and forest habitats on bushes, tall vegetation or in wood rats' nests and raccoons' dens.

Some assassin bug bites, which are painful, cause an allergic, life-threatening reaction in humans. They can also carry a parasite that causes Chagas' disease, common throughout Latin America. The disease is spread by the bug's faeces, which can cause infection when scratched into an open wound or accidentally rubbed into the eye. The disease can kill children by weakening the nervous system and the heart muscle, eventually causing a heart attack. The disease has spread from Mexico to the south of Argentina and has affected 16–18 million people. Fifty thousand die each year.

CASTAWAY

Some species of **mosquito** carry malaria, yellow fever, viral encephalitis or dengue fever. Mosquitoes have killed more people than any other insect. To learn more about mossie nasties, go to page 135.

Leeches wait on vegetation in tropical and damp areas to drop on to you to suck your blood. Remove by applying a pinch of salt or ash, or with fire. These delights can carry infections, so gently squeeze the area and the blood flow will help wash this away. Leave the eventual clot in place to protect the wound.

The **tsetse fly** spreads sleeping sickness. Caused by a parasite, sleeping sickness enters the central nervous system, where it causes deep coma and death. About 250,000 to 300,000 people die each year in Central Africa from sleeping sickness.

There are 20,000 species of **bee**. Bee attacks generally occur when people stumble into a nest or otherwise provoke bees. Africanised honeybees, also known as 'killer bees', are the exception. They were created when African bees were brought to Brazil in 1956 to breed a better honeybee. The effort failed, the bees escaped and they have now killed more than a thousand people, and animals as large as horses as they have moved north through Central America to the southwestern USA. Killer bees swarm all over their victim, delivering an agonising death.

There are also about 20,000 species of **wasp** in the world, including hornets and yellow jackets. Unprovoked wasp attacks are very rare. Wasps usually sting to subdue their prey or in self-defence. People may be stung if wasps have been attracted to their food, or they have inadvertently disturbed a nest. Unlike bees, individual wasps can sting repeatedly.

Eating improperly cooked meat can mean you pick up a little friend to share all your subsequent meals. **Tapeworms** have been known to cause no symptoms for years, but can grow to up to 9 metres (30 feet). **Pinworms**, which lay eggs around the anus and 'migrate' around the surrounding area, can cause sleeplessness, nausea and vomiting, as well as intense itching.

The **hookworm** is a real nasty, found in tropical and subtropical climates, where the inhabitants do not wear shoes or stockings and where the soil is contaminated by human excrement. The larva of the hookworm, living in moist soil or mud, penetrates the exposed skin, usually the sole of the foot, and is then carried by the blood to the lungs. As the larva passes through the lungs, it causes episodes of coughing with bloody sputum. Raised with the mucus into the mouth, the larva is then swallowed. Nice.

Hookworms may also be swallowed with polluted drinking water or with uncleaned vegetables eaten raw. Once ingested, the larva attaches itself with its hooks to the upper portion of the small intestine, where it nourishes itself on the blood of its host, injecting toxins to increase the blood flow at the bite point. The larva matures and the female produces eggs, as many as 30,000 per day, which are passed from the intestine with the faeces, often to contaminate the soil still further. The drain on the blood results in anaemia. This, together with the resulting abdominal pain and diarrhoea, causes general debility. Hookworm, tapeworm and pinworm can all be treated with drugs, but, in their absence, there are other options to try.

Eat a lot of bran, if it's available. This can prevent the parasites getting a hold in the gut. If symptoms appear, eat garlic, pineapple, cloves or pumpkin seeds. You can make an infusion from the leaves of figwort. The Maori made a tea from the roots of bracken.

Apart from washing your hands well, just wear shoes if you can, even if you have to make them yourself out of bark! Apart from hookworm, there is a host of other nasties lurking on the ground in jungle or other tropical areas.

One widespread example is the **jigger** or **chigoe flea**. The smallest known flea, 1mm (or a mere 0.04 inch) long, it is such a poor jumper it can reach a height of only 20cm (8 inches). The breeding female burrows into exposed skin and lays eggs, causing intense irritation. Over about ten days the flea increases in size by 2,000–3,000 times, creating a 5–10mm (0.2–0.4 inch) white lesion with a central black dot, which is the flea's exposed hind legs, respiratory spiracles and reproductive organs. If the flea is left within the skin, severe itching, pain, inflammation and swelling leading to infection may follow.

In North America **chiggers** are **harvest mites**, microscopic relatives of the spider, that inject digestive enzymes into the skin that break down skin cells. They do not actually bite, but instead form a hole in the skin and chew up tiny parts of the inner skin, causing severe irritation and swelling. Intense itching is accompanied by red pimple-like bumps or hives and skin rash or lesions on a sun-exposed area. In East Asia and the South Pacific they can cause scrub typhus. Do not scratch the affected regions. The most effective way to remove chiggers is washing the affected areas with mildly hot water and soap.

Ticks are nasty little buggers, second only to mosquitoes as carriers of infectious and toxic diseases. About the size of a pea, they are blood-sucking parasites often found in tall grass, where they attach themselves to a passing animal with their hypostome, a harpoon-like structure in the mouth that allows them to anchor

themselves in place while sucking blood. Physical contact is their only method of transportation. They will generally drop off when full, but this may take several days.

Hard ticks can transmit relapsing fever, Lyme disease, Rocky Mountain spotted fever, tularaemia, Colorado tick fever and several forms of ehrlichiosis. Symptoms include fever, chills, headaches, pain behind the eyes, light sensitivity, muscle pain, generalised malaise, abdominal pain, nausea and vomiting as well as a flat or pimply rash. While most pass within a few weeks, unless treated promptly Lyme disease (now the second-fastest-growing infectious disease in the US after AIDS) can become a chronic debilitating condition.

It is better to get somebody else to remove the tick as quickly as possible but do not leave the head inside your body, as that may cause infection. Ticks do not like iodine or heat applied to them. Light a match, blow it out and put the hot match head on the tick. Ticks breathe with their back legs, so douse the area in cooking oil or petrol. This should make them back out immediately. Apply fine tweezers as close as possible to the exposed skin and pull upwards with steady, even pressure. Do not puncture the insect's body because its fluids can contain infectious materials. Thoroughly disinfect the bitten area, and wash your hands. If you are within reach of civilisation save the remains in a plastic bag with the date of the bite in case you become ill.

5

SO WE'RE STUCK

CASTAWAY

*'The starved eye devours the seascape for the morsel
Of a sail.*

The horizon threads it infinitely.'

Derek Walcott, 'The Castaway'

After a few days, you've explored your environment and you're sick of sleeping under a log and a blanket of grass. Choosing a permanent campsite is a simple case of location, location, location. And, just as when you're buying a bijou residence in Surbiton, you should spend a great deal of time exploring the options.

Ideally, you want a sheltered spot with a plentiful supply of fresh water and wood for fuel and building materials nearby. Watch for hollows that could become waterlogged, and make sure that your nearest water isn't a breeding ground for ferocious mozzies. Avoid riverbanks, dry watercourses, animal trails and solitary trees, which attract lightning. Check for bees' or hornets' nests and dead wood above, which might come crashing down in a storm. If you choose to remain by the coast make sure that high tides or storms won't come within 50 metres (55 yards). In mountainous areas check there is no evidence of rock slides.

Does moving affect your hopes of rescue, and any signs or pyres you might have already created? Like Crusoe, you might decide that a view of the sea is essential to spot passing ships. If inland, choose flat ground where signals can be laid out.

Prepare your new campsite properly. Imagine you are a town planner and you intend to stay here indefinitely. Is there enough water accessible for drinking and washing? Where will the latrines go? Which is the safest area for the fire? What tools have you got? Will they suffice for building? Have you got enough rope?

⚓ Water and sanitation

It is absolutely essential to keep your drinking water clean. Find a spot with easy access to the stream and a deeper pool. Never wash upstream of this spot. Every couple of days check way upriver to make sure there is nothing nasty polluting the water. Washing your body and clothes should take place further downstream, while cooking utensils should be cleaned even further down as bits of food may attract animals.

Latrines should be situated away from the water source, downhill and downwind of the camp but near enough so that they do get used. Make a path to the latrines and encourage everyone to go down there even if it's just for a pee.

Rather than make like a bear in the woods, dig a trench 1.25 metres (4 feet) deep and 45cm (18 inches) wide. Build up a seat 30–45cm (12–18 inches) high with rocks, logs and dirt and cover with logs, leaving a small hole.

A latrine

A latrine lid

Cover the hole with bark, a flat rock or leaves weighted down with stones. Sprinkle the logs with wood ash to deter flies. Do not waste paper wiping your bum: use leaves, grass or your left hand, as some other cultures do. Never use disinfectant in the pit, because it stops the useful bacteria breaking down your waste material. Cover the faeces with earth and wash your hands immediately. If you have enough containers, keep one filled with water by the toilet. If there is a large group of you, fill in the toilet when it starts to smell or every month to six weeks and burn the seat. Dig a new toilet.

While a urinal isn't absolutely necessary it could help reduce the queues for the latrine if it is a big group. Dig a pit 50cm (20 inches) square and 60cm (2 feet) deep. Fill it with stones three-quarters of the way up and then earth. Make a cone from bark and insert the end into the top layer of stones. Challenge all the other men to an aiming competition.

Rubbish should also be collected downwind of camp and either buried or burned regularly.

Shelters

Always assume that the weather will get worse and build your shelters with facilities for an internal fire. If possible and the wind direction allows, build them facing southeast so that the morning sun will warm the encampment (in the southern hemisphere, build them facing northeast).

Types of shelter

Abandoned buildings/the sod roof

For centuries the coastal Alaskan Inuit living north of the tree line made their 'sod houses' out of salvaged material and whatever else was to hand. Driftwood was tied together to make walls and roof coverings and flat rocks were placed around the sides to give extra stability. The structure was then covered with sods of earth. In winter they cut blocks of snow and piled them high to cover the sides for extra insulation. It needed only a couple of seal-oil lamps to keep a 5-metre-square (16.5-foot-square) house warm and toasty.

If you find abandoned or ruined buildings in the right location say hallelujah — somebody has saved you a lot of effort. Use what remains of the walls as a foundation, then add a sod roof. Start by laying the longest branches you can find across the roof hole — if you're lucky enough to have found bamboo, use that. If you have limited resources, place the strongest branches in the centre, where the roof will be under most pressure.

Where possible, use branches of the same thickness and tied together to create a solid sheet with few gaps. If there is no natural slope to the roof, create one by placing thicker logs in the centre and adding another layer of small branches fanning down. Then lay sods of earth (45cm/17.5 inches by 15 cm/6 inches), or slabs of bark peeled carefully off dead trees (or a combination of the two) on top of the roof.

Don't forget to leave a ventilation hole or your fire will smoke even the hardiest out to face the elements.

CASTAWAY

Bountiful bamboo

During your explorations look out for bamboo clumps. Bamboo is incredibly useful. Not only can it provide a quick drink but it's the most versatile building material you're going to find.

Although officially a grass, it forms a very hard wood that is light and exceptionally tough. It can be used for everything from building and furniture to chopsticks and tattoo needles.

Bamboo grows straight and tall and each stem is divided into culms (hollow cylindrical sections walled at the top and bottom), that can range in height from a few centimetres to 40 metres (130 feet), and from 1mm to 30cm (that's up to a foot) in diameter. Culms may be cut and hollowed into vases or drinking cups, tubes or pipes for liquids.

Bamboo was one of the essential plants carried by Polynesian voyagers when they settled new islands. In the Hawaiian Islands bamboo carried water, made irrigation troughs for taro terraces, was used as a traditional knife for cutting the umbilical cord of a newborn, as a stamp for dyeing bark tapa cloth and for musical instruments. The wood is still used for knitting needles and the fibre can be used for yarn and clothing.

Bamboo shoots are edible and can be stir-fried, boiled with coconut milk or pickled (using the pith of young shoots). The sap of young stalks tapped during the rainy season may be fermented to make *ulanzi* (a sweet wine). The shoots of some species do contain toxins that need to be boiled out before they can be eaten safely.

The hollow sections can also contain fresh, drinkable water – useful if you are out exploring and low on water. First find a small bamboo

shoot about 1cm (0.5 inch) in diameter. Cut it to around 20cm (8 inches) long. Bamboo often has microscopic hairs on the outside, which can irritate the skin, so clean the outside with a leaf or your shirt to get them off. Check that the stem is hollow and clear all the way down. Now you have a drinking straw.

Open up a section of the big bamboo trunk. Make a cut about halfway down the section, and then one a little above it. Without removing your blade from the second cut, twist the knife to pry away the section of the wood between the two cuts. Look into the hole you have just made and you should be able to see some water at the bottom of the section. If there is none, try another section. Smell the water. If it smells bad leave it. Next put your homemade straw into the hole and suck up a little water. If it tastes bad, spit it out; if it tastes nice, drink up!

Wigwam bam

Everyone knows what a wigwam looks like. We've all seen lots of Westerns. Except the conical tent with sticks protruding out of the top is not a wigwam: it's a tepee. The wigwam (or wickiup) is dome-shaped. Glad we've got that sorted.

Both tepees and wigwams make good semipermanent dwelling places. If they were good enough for Geronimo, they're good enough for you.

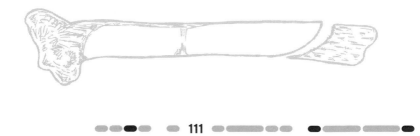

The tepee

The beauty of the classical tepee as used by the Plains tribes lay in its simplicity and flexibility. It was the first mobile home – designed to be set up and struck quickly so that the tribes could follow migrating bison. The long poles protruding out of the top doubled as a travois – pulled by dogs or horses – which held all the family's worldly goods.

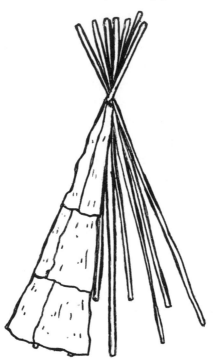

A tepee

There are four elements to the tepee: a set of ten to twenty sapling poles; a canvas, skin or birch-bark cover; an inner lining; and a canvas or skin door. Ropes are used to bind the poles, close the cover, attach the lining and door, while wooden pegs anchor it to the ground. The tepee is the only tent that allows you to have an open fire – thanks to the opening at the top and smoke flaps. The lining provides insulation and supplies a steady, controlled flow of fresh air.

That's the luxury version. Learning how to build the basic tepee shape is a survival essential (it's how you make fires for a start). While it would be nice to have the double-lined Sioux special, a tepee can be constructed very quickly out in the bush and the holes filled with small sticks, stuffed with grass and covered with anything to hand to provide insulation. The angle of the poles acts as a conduit for water – and there's that fire in the middle to keep you snug.

To make a tepee large enough to sleep four to six people you need a long piece of rope and twelve to sixteen poles. The poles, cut from peeled, polished and dried tapered saplings, should measure about 1.8 metres (6 feet) more than the radius of the tepee cover and be about 6.5cm (about 2.5 inches) thick at the base, and 2.5cm (1 inch) thick at the top. They should be as straight and smooth as possible; at the risk of a making a pole-dancing joke, a squaw was rated by the state of her poles – crooked, warped and rough poles were the signs of a slattern.

Start by tying three (some use four because they find it stronger) poles together 3.5 metres (about 12 feet) up, then spread them out in a tripod. One end of the anchor rope is left dangling, long enough to reach the base of the poles. Lay more long poles on to the three primary poles, with their lower ends evenly spaced to form a circle on the ground. The anchor rope is walked around the base of the poles three times and pulled tight. The end of the rope should still reach the ground.

Tie the canvas skin to another pole. The top of the pole rests where all the poles meet. The skin is pulled around the pole framework and pegged to the ground. Move the bases of the non-tripod poles in or out to tension the skin. Inside the tepee, wrap a cord above head height from pole to pole. Suspend the inner lining and peg it near the inside base of the poles. Drive a stout stake inside the tepee, tie the anchor rope to this and the tepee is ready for almost any weather. Dig a hole 45cm (18 inches) wide and 15cm (6 inches) deep for the fire in the centre of the tent. You'll be surprised how a small fire can quickly heat the tepee.

A tepee cover is made by sewing together strips of canvas or hide and cutting out a semicircular shape from the resulting surface. The lining is more difficult to measure, because it's made from strips of canvas assembled to look like a truncated cone. If you don't have the material, improvise. The original tepees used birch bark. If you have limited material, use natural shingle around the outside and hang the material as liner. It doesn't have to be a perfect fit.

Should you be behind enemy lines and happen to come across a parachute, you'll find it makes an excellent cover for a tepee and a perfect fit for a wigwam.

The wigwam

Unlike some Domes, a wigwam should take three days to make and will not cost £800 million and be instantly redundant. It is a practical dwelling because it maximises living space and allows for standing room in the middle. It is easily heated, stable in high winds and relatively simple to build and maintain. The anthropologist Morris Opler recorded how the Chirichua Apache made their wickiups:

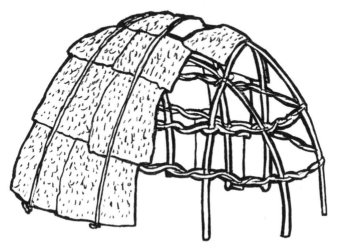

A wigwam

The home in which the family lives is made by the women and is ordinarily a circular, dome-shaped brush dwelling, with the floor at ground level. It is seven feet [2.1 metres] high at the centre and approximately eight feet [2.5 metres] in diameter. To build it, long fresh poles of oak or willow are driven into the ground or placed in holes made with a digging stick. These poles, which form the framework, are arranged at one-foot intervals and are bound together at the top with yucca-leaf strands. Over them a thatching of bundles of big bluestem grass or bear grass is tied, shingle style, with yucca strings. A smoke hole opens above a central fireplace. A hide, suspended at the entrance, is fixed on a cross-beam so that it may be swung forward or backward.

The doorway may face in any direction. For waterproofing, pieces of hide are thrown over the outer hatching, and in rainy weather, if a fire is not needed, even the smoke hole is covered. In warm, dry weather much of the outer roofing is stripped off. The interior is lined with brush and grass beds over which robes are spread ...

(Opler, Morris E, *An Apache Life-way*, University of Nebraska Press, 1994)

None of that is impossible. The tough part is getting the basic dome structure strong and secure. Start with thirty flexible wands or saplings from willow, alder, thin pine or spruce that can be woven together. At the base they should not be much bigger than a thumb-and-forefinger circle. (If the wood is thicker or less flexible, they have to be tied together.) Trim all small branches and foliage off and set aside for later.

A wigwam virgin might want to start by driving a stake into the ground and using a piece of cord to mark a circle. Mark with a sharpened stick where you want the poles to go, half a metre (about 1.5 feet) apart. If the ground is too hard, soften it with water. Holes need to go at least 25cm (10 inches) into the earth.

Use the longest, straightest wands to create long arches over the centre.
Put the ends into the holes and then weave them together in the centre. For
added strength, tie them together. The ceiling should be a full reach taller
than a six-foot person. Stand in the centre and stretch your arm up. For the
side arches bend the poles over two at a time until they meet in the middle.
When the dome structure is in place you add the side bracing – rings of
smaller willow poles about 30cm (1 foot) apart around the sides and top.
Weave any small leafy branches trimmed from your wands into the lattice.

Before adding the covering, bank up all the edges to prevent any surface
water coming in. You can use almost anything for roofing material including
grass, brush, bark, rushes, palm fronds, mats, reeds, animal hides and cloth.
To deflect rain properly you must shingle points where the pitch of the roof
is less than 60 degrees. Native Americans used birch bark, which can be
peeled all year round. The bark of other trees is usually available only from
late spring until midsummer. Boil the bark to make it more flexible and then
sew it into strips.

With the shingle covering in place, make sure it is secured. Either run a
tie-down rope or cord across the dome, or lean logs and poles against the
covering.

The fire will be in the centre of the floor, so make sure there is a hole at the
top of the roof. Keep a piece of shingle to cover the smoke hole when the
fire is not in use.

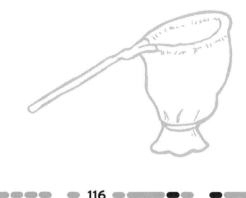

Tools

These shelters can be constructed with little more than a knife and some rope. If you don't have a saw in your survival tin, you can make your own using ends of wire wrapped around two small pieces of wood. Using the toggles as handles pull the wire backwards and forwards in a sawing action.

Ribs from a small animal are ideal for making into a crude needle to sew canvas or bark together. You can use dried animal intestine and fish gut as thread – or you can make your own cord.

Ropes and cords

All you need is one little piece of string – but you don't have it. One sneaker lace is part of the roof and the other melted when it got too close to the fire. Back in the consumer world we use rope, thread and string in every conceivable way but it hardly enters our consciousness. Until we need it. If you're fortunate enough to have a long coil of rope, resist the temptation to cut it to fit. One 5-metre (16.5-foot) rope is potentially far more valuable that five 1-metre (3.3-foot) lengths. By all means use the big rope to tie the corners of your shelter together, but, as soon as you have found an alternative, use that. If you don't have an alternative, make it.

Cordage (as the survival experts prefer to call it) is not used just for tying things up. It can be used for hunting (fishing nets, fishing line, snares and traps), to make bow and bow-drill strings, woven bags and hammocks; you can lash branches together and sew up clothes and wounds.

You can make a line out of bark, animal hair and tendons, vines, grasses or palms. Long plant stems such as vines are only really effective as a short-term, non-load-bearing solution, since they tend to dry out and break. What you need are plant fibres and a lot of patience twisting and plaiting them together.

CASTAWAY

What to look for

Start by looking for the same plants used by industrial rope manufacturers. Different species of agave are grown for sisal and henequen ropes (also, the fermented sap can be distilled into mescal – added worm optional!) and have been successfully planted all over the world. Abaca comes from a species of banana plant. The Maori used raupo and cabbage trees. Any grass that resists crumbling can be made into rope, though it will not be as strong.

Perhaps you can recognise the marijuana plant. Two centuries ago the fields of Britain were covered with hemp plants, which were used to make clothes and ropes for the Royal Navy. Industrial hemp is (un)fortunately non-psychoactive but you can still make cord out of dope plants because you use the fibrous bark from the stem, not the leaves. (It is advisable to smoke the leaves only after you've finished making the rope!)

What you are looking for is a plant with a long stem that's difficult to break by pulling. The fine fibres found just below the skin of the humble stinging nettle are some of the strongest to be found anywhere – and you certainly know when you've found it. For a short-term fix, say making an overnight lean-to shelter using found wood, you could just plait the nettle stems together. It will be strong but not that pliable.

Extracting the fibres

The only way to get at the fibres in some plants (such as flax and fireweed) is by retting – soaking the stalks in water – until the bark peels back. Since this can take a few weeks, you may be better off getting stung, or cannibalising the local yucca.

To get at the fibres in a nettle, first remove all the small stalks and leaves (older browning plants are better than young nettles, whose leaves can be used in soups). Split the main stalk at the top of the plant and peel back the fibres to the leaf joint. Break the stalk above the joint and continue to peel

away the crumbly stem. Try to remove the fibres in two strands. To get rid of any remaining flaky bark, rub each strand between your hands or use one hand and a smooth-barked tree or flat rock. The strands are now lightly rolled and ready for twining (if you want to make a thin fishing line, the strands may have to be further separated).

To extract fibre from agave or yucca plants, look at the base of the plant for partially rotted leaves with intact strong fibres. Take the leaves, find a log or flat rock and beat with another log to separate the fibres. You can use the edge of a knife to expose the threads but that's not as much fun as bashing them. Anyway, the next bit is really picky and fiddly.

And now the cord

Start with a bundle of fibres that is approximately the same thickness as you want your finished rope. Tie them together with an overhand knot – a simple loop and pull. Divide the fibres into two equal bundles. This is really important – if one strand is too much smaller than the other the bigger strand will run straight, the smaller will wrap round it and the strength will be lost.

If you are right-handed, place the knot on top of the index finger of your left hand and let the equal strands hang down both sides. Next, hold it securely and twist the fibres with your right hand. Twist the fibres of one strand and then the other – twist in the same direction – with your left index finger keeping the two strands apart. Hold on tight with your right hand because the fibres want to unravel and you don't want that. As you remove your left finger, all that suppressed energy and tensions causes the strands close to the knot end to twist around each other, forming the beginning of your cord.

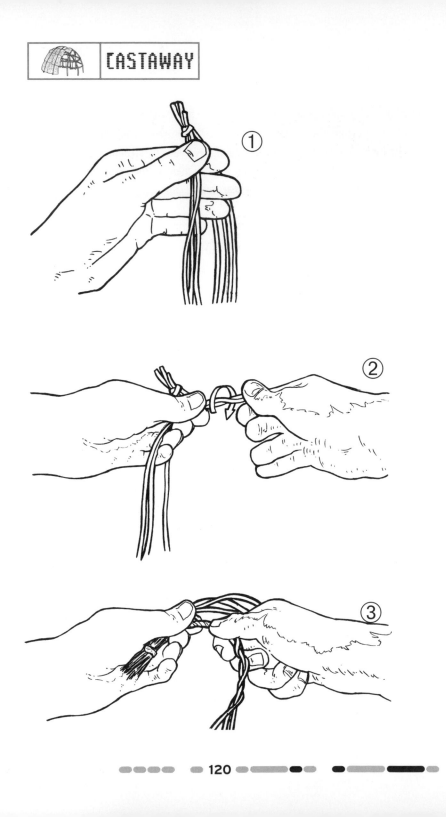

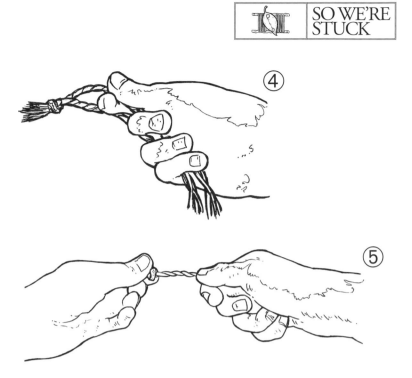

Next, give the strands a helping twist with your right hand to increase tension in the cord. Push your left index finger to separate the strands again and on you go, adding maybe a centimetre (0.5 inch) to the cord with each pass. If you need to make a longer piece of cord and the fibres are not long enough, you can lay other fibres on the others and twist them right in. Make sure the new fibres are the same thickness as the original and stagger where you add the new fibres in the strand. Two joints in the same place will weaken the cord. Trust the feeling in your fingers. They will know what your eyes may deny. Add the new fibres by laying them along the old. The harder the strands are twisted and the steeper the twist angle, the stronger and stiffer the cord becomes. To make a cord 4mm (about 0.2 inch) thick you must make two twists per centimetre; for a cord half a millimetre (a mere 0.02 inch) thick you must make twelve twists. See what we mean about taking time? As you get better and require stronger cordage, try twining three strands of fibre instead of two. The resulting three-ply cord will be almost twice as strong as the two-ply.

To finish off, roll your completed cord between two flat surfaces or boards. This smoothes it out and evens out any minor inconsistencies in the twist. Rubbing it back and forth also raise any surface fibres. The ends can be trimmed off with a sharp knife or singed off in the fire when you have finished. Just be careful not to set fire to your brand new rope.

Using your cord

Making your own rope is a long but ultimately satisfying process. The more you do it the nimbler your fingers and the more more impressive the final product will become. Use homemade cord for binding objects, tying off cooking spits or lashing roof planks together. Unless you are totally confident in the strength of your rope, do not use it to scale cliffs or explore caves.

Keep your cord dry – especially fishing lines and fishing nets. Prolonged exposure to water rots the fibres and seawater is particularly corrosive. Nobody wants the big one to get away because the line breaks.

Where to site the campfire

Fire is potentially lethal – especially if the ground and vegetation are dry. It doesn't take much for a spark from a carelessly positioned fire to ignite the bush. In a few minutes the flames could take everything you own, destroy shelters you have spent days building and send the wildlife fleeing. The ground will recover but you may not. Severe burns are hard to treat even in a hospital. Out in the wild, the options are agony, permanent disfigurement and death.

So think safe when you locate your fire – even if it has been raining pachyderms and wombats for days. Choose a site that is big enough to sit around singing 'Kum-Bay-Ya' (just joking – but only about the choice of song). The fire will be the communal centre of the camp, so make sure it feels comfortable – a good view of the sun setting over the sea helps. The campfire might also double as a signal fire but for that you need something that will sent a sheet of flame in the air – and that should not be next to your homes.

When space is not an issue, build a separate cooking fire by digging a
trench 35 by 100cm (14 by 39 inches) and 35–40cm (14–16 inches) deep.
Carpet the floor of the trench with flat-topped rocks and light the fire along
the rocks. When the fire dies down the rocks will remain hot enough to cook
on, and it's easy to have a small spit for roasting over the embers. This
trench fire is safer and much easier to cook on.

If possible, build the fire on a sand or gravel base. Once you have chosen
the fire site, clear away any leaves, twigs, pine needles, moss and dried
grass, leaving a 3-metre (10-foot) circle of bare earth. If the ground is
dry, dig out the duff until you reach mineral soil. Duff is the layer of
decomposing materials that resides between the mineral soil and the litter
layer of fallen twigs, needles and leaves in woodland. It is really important
to make sure there is nothing that can ignite.

You can surround the fire with rocks. This will retain heat, save fuel and
provide stands for heating cooking pots. Bang them together and discard
any that sound hollow or crack. Avoid slates and soft rocks and do not use
wet rocks, as the heat can cause them to crack and even explode.

Indoors, heat from a fire reflects off the walls to warm the whole room.
Outside, only surfaces facing a campfire are warmed by it, so the heat
quickly dissipates. If you site the fire near a large boulder the rock will
reflect the heat and warm your back. You can also build a reflector – as
simple as a log pile 60–90cm (2–3 feet) tall – which reflects heat back on to
you and pushes the smoke straight up. A reflector positioned opposite the
entrance to your shelter will help heat the inside.

Fires inside shelters
Until you get experience at both building shelters and making fires, be wary
of mixing the two. Get it wrong and you could end up with no shelter, no kit
and no hair.

If the shelter is fully enclosed, the fire can be smaller – but make sure there is ventilation for the smoke to escape. Lay a 'parallel' fire with logs cut into shorter lengths and laid in straight line. In a large enclosed shelter you can burn long logs placed in a very open star shape (picture a wagon wheel with no rim) with bodies sleeping between them. Just raise the end of the logs to prevent the fire travelling along them and push them inwards as they burn.

Making sense of chaos: ten camp rules

1. Keep food covered, raised or suspended off the ground.
2. Keep your kit in a dry place well away from the fire.
3. Never leave the fire unattended.
4. When leaving the camp, travel in pairs.
5. Do not prepare game in the camp. If you have caught an animal in a trap, gut it there, since that will attract other game to the traps, not to the camp.
6. Keep busy and share nasty jobs.
7. Routines are important – have a meeting at a set time every day.
8. Have set times for leisure.
9. Encourage games, singing and storytelling; include everyone who wants to be included.
10. Respect privacy and personal space.

6

I'M HUNGRY
(AND HE'S GREEDY)

CASTAWAY

On an island there is one source of food available 24/7 – the sea. You have already gathered seaweed and bivalves, but fish are a valuable source of protein. You just have to catch them. However, if water is short – you're rationed to less than a pint a day – do not eat fish, or anything else (see page 31).

Fishing with a rod is very sporting but catching one at a time after hours of waiting is not very effective time management. That said, if you do have the time and enough supplies back at camp it is very therapeutic to drowse on the riverbank or seashore. Short of dynamite or poison, it doesn't matter what means you use to catch fish – the essential requirement is patience. Fish are naturally wary, for they are all a link in someone else's food chain.

Freshwater streams can provide more than fish. Crayfish can be found in fast-running, stony-bottomed parts of streams and shrimps in slower-moving water with vegetation around its edges. Dig around in the silt for freshwater mussels. Eels favour the cover of boulders, overhanging banks and deep pools. Mostly nocturnal, they're best caught using traps. Small fish, whitebait-sized, favour gently flowing pools and runs. Bigger freshwater fish hide under boulder-overhung banks or beneath woody debris.

The sea will have a much wider variety to choose from but there's also a lot of ocean to escape into. Different species have specific habitats. A reef with adjacent sand or shell habitats will be home to snapper, tarakihi, goatfish and blue cod. The shores of New Zealand's islands play host to such wonderful names as triplefins, black angelfish, clown toady, black-spotted goatfish and, best of all, the toadstool groper.

Dawn and dusk are usually the best times for river fish. In hot weather, just like humans, they will move to shady places or deep water. When it is cold they seek a shallow, warm spot. They look for shelter under banks and rocks and feel secure under white water where the turbulence renders them invisible. Look for spots where the water flows through a narrow gap or gushes over rocks. Fish often feed before a storm, so, if you've been cloud watching and feel the weather changing, it is a good time to try your luck.

Just as you would when stalking ground game, approach fishing sites slowly and cautiously. Fish can see figures walking up to a riverbank, hear noise, feel vibration and will buzz off on the slightest pretext. If you are spear-fishing on a sunny day, do not approach the fish with the sun behind you, the moment your shadow falls on the water they're off and your language will match the colour of the sea.

At the risk of going all Zen, you need to feel at one with the environment. Watch the water. Ring ripples breaking on the surface or flashes of silver followed by a splash indicate feeding. If the fish start biting when a particular insect is close to the surface, try to catch that. Bait can be anything: live maggots, worms, insects, shellfish, shrimps, tiny fish. Do not be squeamish about using live bait as its movement will attract the fish.

Chuck a handful of bait into the water and see what reaction it gets, then try a different type until you get the yummy response. In the sea, if you see shoals of little fish darting all over the place they are probably being pursued by a bigger predator. If big fish like eating a particular little fish, catch some of them first.

Nets, lines and hooks

Women's tights make a very effective makeshift net for minnows. If a pair of fishnets are available, beg for them very nicely, pray there are no ladders and land something bigger. (Don't underestimate the nutritional value of tiny fish. Catch enough, boil or dry them and eat them whole.) To make a simple fishing net, find a forked stick. Thread the forks through the hem of the bottom of an old T-shirt. When the ends meet, push them out through a hole and tie them together with string. Tie off the armholes and neck hole to make the base of the net secure.

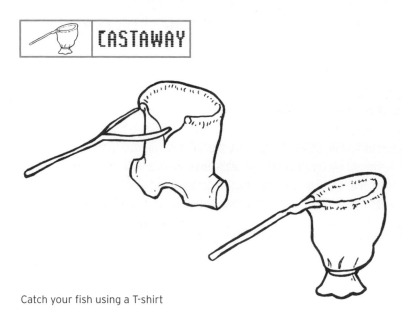

Catch your fish using a T-shirt

Once you have caught a fish, inspect its insides for a clue as to what it really likes to eat. Then bait your hook with it, drop it in the water, then scatter a few morsels on top to encourage the fish. Worms, maggots, grasshoppers, beetles and small fish are generally popular with river fish; in the sea, small chunks of meat or other small fish are the best bait. For a minnow, the hook needs to be placed towards the tail, pushed through the body and under the backbone; the line will need a float to keep the bait off the bottom.

If you have line and fishing hooks and want to use a rod, any springy sapling will do, but without a reel you will have to rely on waiting for the bite, striking hard to embed the barbs and playing the fish until it is exhausted.

Making hooks is easier than it might appear. Stiff wire, safety pins or paper clips can all be fashioned into effective hooks. Just make sure there is a strong loop to tie the line to. You could even try using wood. Find a green hardwood branch with a strong fork in it. Whittle the wood away, keeping a natural curve, and sharpen the end to a point. If all else fails, try the sharp thorns you blundered into when exploring.

Fishing-line knots

The fisherman's knot (see page 72) is not always effective when you're using thin nylon line. Try the half-blood knot. Thread an end through the eye of the hook. Make four turns along the line, then pass the live end back through the first loop formed next to the hook. Pull tight and snip off the end. To join two pieces of nylon together use a double threefold half-blood knot. Lay the lines facing each other. Twist one three times around the other and bring the end back and pass it through where the two lines cross. Repeat on other line. The two ends should be facing in opposite directions. Gently pull tight.

Most anglers have floats in their kit. When the hook takes a bite, the float disappears rousing you from stupor into action. Make your own by tying the line around a piece of cork, bark or wood. Don't make it too big or it could get in the way. If you have a survival tin you will have stored split lead shot with the fishing hooks. Attaching them will stop the line trailing on the surface of the water and keep the bait moving. If your fish seem to prefer a deeper life, attach a heavier weight at the bottom then run your hook off 10–15cm (4–6 inches) higher up the line. Fish, especially barracuda, are also attracted to bright shiny objects in the water. A buffed-up Yale key, or silver paper from cigarette packets or chocolate wrappers can make an enticing lure.

Certain fish, particularly crustaceans, are nocturnal. They are attracted to light, so if you have a net and a torch you're in business. The water needs to be still. Place the net under water and then point the torch on to the surface. When the fish arrive draw the net up, trapping the fish so you can spear or club them. The same principle works if you place a mirrored surface on the bottom of a river or the ocean floor. The mirror will reflect sunlight and moonlight, attracting the fish.

One hook equals one bite – maximum. Setting a trap line of six hooks, each with a juicy worm wriggling away, increases your chances of landing supper. Attach one end of the trap line to a heavy rock, then attach lines with baited hooks at regular intervals (make sure that the lines are not so long that they get tangled up). Just before dusk, drop the rock into the water, making sure it is resting on the bottom and won't move. Pull taut and secure the line's end to a post, a tree or an even larger immoveable rock on the land. Go to bed. Check the line in the morning, and land, cook and eat fresh fish. Of course you can keep it there all day but check it at frequent intervals and replace the bait when it's stopped wriggling.

Fish traps

Creating artificial shelters and hiding places attracts and concentrates fish. You can make a brush trap by tying branches, sticks and brush into bundles. Lay them flat or upright on the bottom if it's shallow or suspend them in the water. Fish and crustaceans sheltering in the brush trap can be caught by quickly lifting the bundles from the water.

Set tubes for eels and other long thin fish to use as shelter. The tube should be closed at one end and can be made from bamboo, hollow logs or plastic bottles and pipe tied into groups of two. Place bait inside the tubes to attract the eels or fish. When lifting the tubes, take care that the eels do not escape, as they are very slippery customers.

In a shallow stream where you have seen several fish you can create a one-way cul-de-sac. First build a rectangular pen either by piling up rocks or pushing sticks vertically into the river bottom. Then build a 'V'-shaped wedge. The centre of the 'V' should be open but narrow and right in the middle of the pen. The pen should, if possible, cover the width of the stream. Then walk 100 metres (about 110 yards) upstream and come back down through the stream, herding the fish into the 'V'. They will come to the apex, turn either left or right and be trapped. If the trap is really well situated and secure, consider blocking the exit and using it as a holding tank.

The basic principle for all fish traps is to channel the fish into a narrow opening that is very hard for them to get back out of. Lobster and crab pots follow the same principle. They can be made by laths of timber, cane or bamboo rods or steel mesh. In northeastern Brazil, rock lobster pots are traditionally made from mangrove sticks.

For an all-purpose fish trap, weave and tie wicker, or use hazel and willow saplings, bamboo or thick reeds, in a torpedo shape with a wide opening and slats narrowing into a much smaller hole. Tie bait two-thirds of the way down the torpedo. Place it on the bottom of a stream or shallow sea bed so that the current is flowing through the open mouth. Fish think it's another piece of debris.

A more effective lobster pot needs to be conical in shape. It rests on the bottom and the lobsters come in through the top searching for bait and then cannot climb out again. To make them you do need a round piece of board at the top with holes bored into it. If this is too difficult to make with found material, experiment with a bigger torpedo.

Making a conical lobster pot

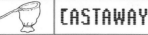
Bait is normally secured in the catching chamber of the trap or pot. Large, solid pieces of fish, animal bone or small animals are tied into the pot with wire or twine. If small pieces of bait such as small fish or chicken heads are used, they should be placed in a bait container to hold them together and in place. This is effective when the bait is extremely attractive.

⌐ Spearing and tickling

If you've been cast away on a deserted island, chances are that the sea fish are as yet unfamiliar with their most dangerous predator. You should take advantage of this by trying to spear them. Neptune, the god of the sea, had a point – or rather three, because he always carried a trident. A three-pronged spear increases your chances of getting a hit and a wounded fish will not go very far.

Spearing fish is not easy. Be prepared to spend many fishless, curse-packed hours practising. First, find an area where there are lots of fish and wait for them to get used to your presence. Stab directly downwards, don't throw. If the spear enters the water at an angle the refraction of the water will disturb your aim. You can use a bow in the same way but make longer arrows for fishing and try to put a barb on the arrowhead.

In a clear, moving stream, try tickling for trout. They are very nervous fish and try to conceal themselves beneath cover such as undercut banks, rocks and logs, preferably under overhanging branches, where they can wait for insects to drop. It takes time and patience and you do need to be relaxed for when you encounter a fishy body. If you start, he's gone.

Lie on the bank, roll up your sleeve and dip your hand in to bring it to water temperature. Work gradually upstream gently probing for fish under the bank. The first thing you will meet will be flapping tail. Stroke it gently a few times, then move the strokes up the body gently, softly as you go. Once your hand is under the gills flick the fish quickly on to the bank, rolling your body back at the same time. The trout only has to thrash a couple of feet in the right direction to be back in the water, so move quickly to pin it to the ground, then hit it on the head. If you stand up to show off your prize, it will probably wriggle free into the water.

Yes, it is even harder to do than it sounds!

✐ Gutting and cooking fish

Once you've landed a fish hit it on the head with a rock or a club. Now eat it as soon as possible. In the heat it goes off quickly. Anything under 5cm (2 inches) long can be eaten whole and you won't notice the bits.

For bigger fish, take your knife and just behind the head hold the gill flaps open and cut the gills out. Then slit the belly open from anus to gills and scrape out the innards, which make very good bait. Freshwater fish roe, small tiny eggs that run down the side, is nutritious and tasty, so don't bin it. Wash the body cavity thoroughly in fresh water. Scaling and beheading the fish are optional. Fish heads make good bait, but leaving the head on and inserting a stick between the gills makes it easier to spit-roast.

If you're baking a whole fish in embers, keep the scales on, as they will protect the skin from burning too quickly and will then fall off. If you do want to scale a fish, lay it flat and, as you run the back of a knife blade or a credit card from tail to head, the scales will ping off. If your eel trap has caught you a whopper, you will want to skin it. Cut skin around the neck then pull down towards the tail.

Saltwater fish can be eaten raw, especially when it's still wriggling. Sushi and sashimi are deeply delicious, but they are cut from larger fish with huge chunks of flesh by chefs who know what they are doing. Freshwater fish can contain parasites, so should be cooked through.

You can eat everything except the innards. If you are hungry enough, you can eat the eyes, brain and heart, but avoid the liver, intestines, or the

roe of tropical fish. Stomach contents (a large fish might have ingested a sardine) may or may not be edible, depending on how digested they are and how hungry you are. In any case, you will need to wash them to get rid of stomach acids. Taste them carefully.

Don't waste anything. If you are short of water, you'll be glad to know that the eye and the area around it usually contains a lot of moisture. The cheeks have a small amount of particularly tasty meat. Scrape and suck the inside of the skin to get the benefit of any fat stores there. If anything is left, dry it to use later.

Don't overcook fish, because it loses its taste very quickly; but there are few things to beat a freshly caught trout baked in the embers. And as Bertie Wooster liked to remark, fish is good for the brain.

Fish recipes

Angelfish
The angelfish looks similar to rays in that its body is flattened. Its rough, tough skin can be used to polish wood, and as a lining for sheaths for knives or machetes. The best part is the tail end, which should be simmered over the fire – ideally with sautéed parsley, carrot, celery, garlic, and onion and tomato-infused water – for ten minutes per 2.5cm (1 inch) of thickness of the fish.

Lobster
Split their tails lengthwise with a large knife. Brush the flesh with oil and lemon juice, preferably seasoned with salt, paprika, white pepper and garlic powder. Place them meat-down over the fire for a few minutes, then turn over and cook for about six minutes, brushing with the lemon-oil-seasoning mixture. The lobster is done when it is opaque and firm to the touch.

✒ Scurvy

Ferdinand Magellan's ship the *Victoria* was the first vessel to sail around the world in 1519–21. His crew were also the first to report the symptoms of scurvy. During their epic voyage, fresh food ran out and the crew were thrown back on their decayed biscuit supplies, and then reduced to eating leather and rats. 'As a result of this bad nourishment, a strange disease fell upon us. The upper and lower gums swelled so greatly as to cover the teeth, so that the sick man could take no good.' (Sue Shephard, *Pickled, Potted and Canned: The story of food preservation*, Headline, 2000) The surviving men recovered with great speed once they were able to take on board fresh coconuts, yams and sugar cane.

As ships' crews became larger, it was found impossible to take enough fresh food, and scurvy became the most feared enemy of the Royal Navy. Of the 185,000 men raised for sea service during the Seven Years War (1756–63), 130,000 are reported to have died of scurvy.

It is an extreme form of vitamin C deficiency. Existing only on a diet of fish, which do not provide vitamins, you will be subject to scurvy and anaemia. In a few weeks your mouth may begin to hurt. To ensure you get enough vitamin C, try to eat some citrus fruit or potatoes if they are available.

SHIT HAPPENS! Deadly diseases

The mosquito has a lot to answer for. Certain species carry diseases that have slaughtered humans for centuries. The most deadly is **malaria**. Caused by a parasite that is transmitted to humans through the bites of the infected *Anopheles* genus of mosquito, malaria remains a huge scourge, killing someone in the world every thirty seconds. The parasites migrate to the liver and then infect red blood cells, where they multiply, rupturing the cells, and then spreading further. The weakening and disruption of the body's blood results in uncontrolled shivering, chattering teeth, high fever, sweating and a burning thirst, headaches, nausea and vomiting, muscle pain and anaemia. This can lead to jaundice, convulsion, coma, rupture of the spleen and subsequent massive haemorrhage. If you live, you are severely weakened physically, and prone, as an aftereffect, to debilitating depression. Malaria attacks confer no instant immunity and can recur in those who survive, often killing on the third or fourth attack.

Yellow fever is an almost uniquely distressing, disgusting and terrifying disease. There is still no cure, apart from treating the symptoms of the disease, such as kidney failure. If you do survive, you are at least immune. It's caused by an arbovirus, a small virus transmitted by the bites of certain mosquitoes, and early symptoms include headaches, loss of appetite, and muscle pain. A high temperature follows, accompanied by severe back pain, which many have described as like being on the rack. After that comes a burning, agonising thirst, the telltale jaundice as the face and eyes yellow, and the dreaded '*vomito negro*' – throwing up choking mouthfuls of dark blood, as the virus causes liver and kidney failure and multi-organ dysfunction and haemorrhage. The brain can be affected, producing delirium, seizures and coma. The medical shock, caused by extreme fluid loss, can be fatal.

It doesn't stop there. Mosquitoes can also transmit **dengue fever**. This lasts about a week, causing joint pains, a skin rash and severe headaches. If you pick up one of the nastier strains, it can lead to fatal hemorrhagic disease. This disease is experiencing something of a renaissance at the moment. There is no cure. Rest and fluids are all that you can administer. Do *not* give aspirin, since it increases the internal bleeding.

When you are cast away, you can expect to suffer what is euphemistically called 'runny tummy'. There are a number of herbal remedies for diarrhoea, including an infusion of hazel, bramble or mint leaves, a decoction of oak or elm bark (you can make a decoction by boiling the bark) or an infusion of plantain leaves and stems. Most important is to keep hydrated. However, it could get worse.

Dysentery was once known as 'the bloody flux' because, alongside the severe diarrhoea, there is blood in the runs. The disease is caused by ingesting food or water containing microorganisms, which inflame the intestines, bringing abdominal pain, fever and – *ouch!* – rectal pain. It spreads like wildfire and can cause death from liver failure. Among its famous victims are Epicurus, Henry V and Sir Francis Drake. Just as the runs can foreshadow dysentery, cold or flu symptoms could be working themselves up to **pneumonia**. This is an illness of the lungs and respiratory system in which the alveoli (microscopic air-filled sacs of the lung responsible for absorbing oxygen from the atmosphere) become inflamed and flooded with fluid. Pneumonia can result from a variety of causes, including infection with bacteria, viruses, fungi or parasites.

People with infectious pneumonia often cough up a greenish or yellow sputum and suffer a high fever accompanied by shaking chills. Shortness of breath is also common, as is a sharp or stabbing chest pain, during deep breaths or coughs. They may also cough up blood, experience headaches or develop sweaty and clammy skin. Other symptoms include loss of appetite, fatigue, blueness of the skin (due to lack of oxygen in the blood), nausea, vomiting, and joint pains or muscle aches. It can lead to acute respiratory distress and death, especially among the elderly and people who are chronically ill. One in three newborn deaths is down to pneumonia. In 1918 Sir

William Osler, known as 'the father of modern medicine', described pneumonia as the 'captain of the men of death'.

In the absence of drugs, the general advice for these diseases is to deal with the symptoms and try to keep the victim as cheerful and comfortable as possible. To 'break' a fever by inducing perspiration, give the patient camomile or elder tea. Or you can make an infusion out of elm bark, elder flowers or lime flowers. Tea made of willow leaves and bark contains salicin, an important part of aspirin. Rest and liquids are vital. So is getting the hell out and into hospital.

When groups go wrong

'Because the rules are the only thing we've got!'

Ralph in William Golding's *Lord of the Flies*

Whereas Defoe's *Robinson Crusoe* demonstrates the nobility and ingenuity of the castaway, William Golding captures the fragility of civilisation and shows how fear of the unknown can destroy it. In *Lord of the Flies* evil comes from within, or, more precisely, from the failure of the group. Early on, the boys are full of optimism, and expect the island to be fun, despite the fact that many of them are scared of a 'Beastie' – a dangerous wild animal on the island allegedly seen by one of the younger boys who has a birthmark on his face. From the very start, another boy, Piggy, is marked out by his asthma and corpulence as an outcast.

The boys then make their first attempt at being rescued by starting a signal fire (lit with the help of Piggy's glasses). The fire burns out of control, and scorches half of the island. The boy who first saw the 'Beastie' goes missing during the fire, and is never seen again.

Life on the island deteriorates, becoming more disorganised as the two strongest characters (Jack and Ralph) vie for leadership. They have conflicting aims for the island, and only Ralph and another character, Simon, are willing to build shelters.

Descent into chaos starts, ironically, when the possibility of rescue by a passing ship is missed. Jack had led a group off hunting, taking with him the boys who were tending to the signal fire, so the ship sailed past. An intense argument ensues, with Ralph trying to establish the precedence of group over individual interest. Although the signal fire is maintained along with a false sense of security, the order among the boys quickly deteriorates as Jack and Ralph continue their power struggle.

The landing of a dead man by parachute turns the low-level fear into a contagion of panic when it is assumed he is the 'Beastie'. Jack leaves the group to create a new tribe, followed by most of the older boys. In Jack's tribe, where fear and superstition go unchecked, the beast comes to seem more and more real until its existence is an article of faith. Jack, who gains his authority by promising he'll protect the others from the beast, succumbs to the fear himself.

This new tribe hunt down a pig, and decide to host a feast. Before that, they sever the pig's head and place it on a stick as an 'offering' to the Beastie. Flies swarm around the head of the pig. Simon comes across it, and, overcome with horror and fear, he imagines that the head talks to him. Its message foreshadows Simon's fate. He runs down from the mountain to tell the others about being spoken to by the 'Lord of the Flies'. However, he is mistaken for the Beastie, and beaten to death by the other boys.

Ralph's tribe dwindle in number. Jack's larger, less civilised tribe, however, need to steal from Ralph's to maintain their existence. They steal Piggy's glasses to light a fire. Piggy demands his glasses back, but is killed when Roger launches a boulder into him, sending him over a cliff. Jack tries and fails to kill Ralph, and the next day his tribe try to hunt him down to murder him.

CASTAWAY

If you are aware enough about how groups work to establish rules and procedures from the outset and to guard against 'contagion', then you will avoid the fate of the boys in *Lord of the Flies*. However, because group structures are constantly evolving and not set in stone, problems will arise. Time spent together can nourish the group, creating shared experience. But it can also lead to dissolution and disaster.

United we stand

Unless things stay fair, you're heading for trouble. It was inequality – of resources and jobs – that led to the bloodbath on Pitcairn Island. Less dramatically, arguments arise when it is felt that one of the group is not pulling their weight. Don't be surprised by this: it pretty much always happens. In a tug-of-war team the more people there are in the group, the less individual effort nearly all of them make. Psychologists call this *social loafing*. If it becomes a real problem, have one person clearly responsible for one thing within the task.

In *Lord of the Flies*, chorister Jack had a ready-made subgroup, which he steered for his personal benefit against the interest of the group. Subgroups are where rebellion against the main group's rules is nurtured. No one likes 'cliquiness', but don't be surprised when subgroups form; if the group is over thirty strong, it is inevitable. Even in smaller groups, when people click they naturally band together for mutual support. Think of teenage girls meeting each other for the first time: they both like the same band, and suddenly it's instant rapport, with the added bonus of discovering they both hate their parents.

Subgroups will develop around people or ideas but, provided that they are not in direct conflict to the objectives of the whole group, this needn't be the end of the world. It may be the beginning of a new one, as most new ideas and inspirations tend to come from small groups.

Scapegoating

In the Bible the scapegoat was an animal that was ritually laden with the sins of the village and then driven into the wilderness to die, thus cleansing the people of that month's particular bad behaviour. It has come to mean those who are blamed for not only their own faults but for the faults of others as well.

Scapegoats fall broadly into two categories: the willing and the different. The willing become victims because they expect to be treated badly by others and so are. For them, being the butt of group wrath is preferable to being ignored. The different are selected by the crowd because their appearance, age, beliefs or habits stand out or because they do not conform.

To be rejected by a group can be crushing. It is easy to ignore one person's bitching and tendency to blame you for everything by dismissing it as bias. But it is much more difficult to resist the same response from a number of people at the same time. Curiously, though, scapegoating can benefit the group. Studies have shown that the scapegoat draws off so much bad feeling, it frees everybody else to work more productively and harmoniously.

Incomers

When a new person arrives the dynamic alters. They are exciting but also threatening and need to be socialised, be made to understand the aims and culture of the group. Initiation rites – face painting, naked swimming – are common, and can be fun, embarrassing or brutal. While you must avoid humiliating the new member in general, the harder the 'rites' are, the more the person will feel they have invested in the group and the more they will bring to it. It's also a good excuse for a party.

Positive thinking and trust

When groups go wrong you want to discover why. A postmortem becomes dangerous if it degenerates into apportioning blame. The secret is to analyse your successes as well as your failures. As Bing Crosby sings, 'Accentuate the positive'.

CASTAWAY

Imagine some of the more passive members of the group are feeling left out of the decision-making process. The group, as a whole, is getting bored. Have a brainstorming session. OK, this does sound like the stuff they do in poncy ad agencies trying to come up with an idea for selling liquefied manure to club-goers. But try it. You could be surprised not only by the ideas but the effect it has on the group

The gist is to produce as many novel or creative ideas as possible. Jim suggests having a party every full moon; Anna suggests you build a special oven for a feast; Danni wants dancing; Tom says he knows how to make drums. Jim's original idea has been built on by other group members and come full circle. The central tenet of brainstorming is that no idea is bad and so no idea should be criticised or evaluated. Agree set rules and a time limit. Don't hold back. Offer ideas that come to mind with no discussion, comment or detail; build on others' ideas; encourage or ensure that every member of the group is able to contribute equally.

Unless you are brain dead, brainstorming is enjoyable and thought-provoking; it encourages the sharing of ideas, reduces dependency on a single authority figure; and it encourages interaction. Just make sure you listen when the quietest mouse opens their mouth. You may be surprised.

There are other fun ways to build understanding, trust and creativity in a group. Yes, it's touchy-feely time. Draw lots to find a partner. Take it in turns to fall backwards so the partner can catch you. Or try the 'blind walk' in which one person leads another blindfold, without talking, for ten minutes – and then reverse roles. Better still, involve the whole group. One member stands in the centre of a close circle, eyes closed, and sways to and fro, supported by a gradually widening circle. Try the 'body lift', in which each member of the group is lifted to a horizontal position above the heads of the group. The elevated person must relax and close their eyes until they are lowered gently to the ground. Alternatively form two lines and gently pass the person along the line at head height. However tempting it might be, do not drop somebody deliberately!

These games may seem silly, but they perform vital functions. Role playing gives group members security in which to express themselves, and creates an open, accepting atmosphere in which mistrust and hostilities are broken down. Where there is no trust, war follows.

SHIT HAPPENS! Deadly fish

Paralytic shellfish poisoning usually comes from eating mussels, cockles or clams that have eaten poisonous dinoflagellates. These tiny, single-cell marine organisms are the critters that make up a red tide, but they can make sea animals poisonous even if there are not enough of them around to make a red tide. Red tides are found mostly in the temperate latitudes between March and November in the northern hemisphere and September and May in the southern hemisphere. Symptoms of poisoning start with tingling or burning in the lips, mouth and face. This then spreads over the entire body, with the tingling becoming numbness, and the numbness – sometimes – paralysis. Victims usually feel dizzy, weak and very thirsty, with aching joints, excessive saliva and difficulty swallowing. There is no treatment beyond vomiting it up as quickly as possible.

Do not touch any fish that looks like a stone, puffs up or has barbed teeth. Do not pick up any pointed, spindle-shaped shells. Most fish that sting live on the seabed. The pain of a sting is intense, but few people die except from stonefish and stingray wounds. The pain may last only a few hours, but it could be the worst pain you'll ever experience.

The **scorpion fish** makes for great eating, but has nasty poisonous spines located on the head and fins. Its venom remains dangerous even after death, so dispose of the carcass carefully. Be warned that they can survive out of the water for up to an hour.

Stonefish are deadly. They lie in shallow pools and are found off India, China and Australia and across the South Pacific. They are almost impossible to spot, and, if you tread on one, the dorsal spines will inject a ferocious poison that is agonising and generally fatal.

Stingrays have a barbed stinger on their tail. They mostly live on the sea floor. If one takes your line, cut it and donate the hook to the sea. Contrary to popular belief, stingrays are not predators. They have only small mouths with two hard flat plates, which they use to catch crabs and molluscs. If disturbed, rays will explode out of the sand and flee with great speed. They are not aggressive, but if cornered will lash out with the serrated barbs at their base of their tales. Steve 'Crocodile Hunter' Irwin was killed in September 2006, when a barb pierced his heart.

If you are caught by a stingray barb, do not use a tourniquet. Put the injured part in the hottest water you can stand for thirty minutes. The heat breaks down the poison. It is particularly important to treat the victim for shock by elevating the feet and keeping warm. Lacerations should be washed in salt water.

Moray eels live in holes in the rocks. The slime around their mouths is poisonous and wounds fester for ages. Nasty.

Sea snakes are the world's most abundant reptile. There are more than fifty species of sea snake, and they can be found anywhere the water is warm, and in some cold places as well. They feed on the bottom, but have to come to the surface to breathe. Most are around a metre (3.3 feet) long, but some grow up to 3 metres (10 feet).

If one bites on your line, cut it. Sea snake venom is more toxic than that of a king cobra. One drop of their poison can kill three men.

They bite with small fangs like a cobra, injecting up to eight drops of venom. After the bite, it doesn't seem so bad. An hour later the symptoms begin to emerge – aching and anxiety, sometimes combined with mild euphoria; then the aching gets worse, as the tongue feels thick and unwieldy. Paralysis starts in the legs and works its way up the torso, as the pulse gets weaker and weaker. Nausea, vomiting, spasms and increasingly severe convulsions can be followed by unconsciousness and death.

About a third of sea-snake bites are fatal. If no antivenin is available, keep the wound below the level of the heart, restrict the movement of the affected limb and avoid all exertion. Keep the victim as warm and calm as possible. Have them drink water but not alcohol. Hope for the best.

Jellyfish should all be treated as poisonous, although only a few are really dangerous. The symptoms of jellyfish stings range from a prickly rash though to cramps, nausea, respiratory problems, paralysis, convulsions and death.

If you are stung first pull the jellyfish off, using gloved hands, a stick, seaweed or whatever else comes to hand. Jellyfish tentacles have millions of venom-injecting cells, and those cells keep firing as long as the tentacle is in contact with the body. Treating the stings thereafter depends on what you have. Alcohol – at last a medical use! – is the best. Pour it over the skin or pat it on with a wet cloth. This dilutes the venom and reduces the amount that gets into your system. But do not apply the alcohol before all tentacles are removed, as this would only make it worse. If you have antihistamine pills, now is the moment to take them. Otherwise, onion juice or strong black tea can be applied to the sting to help alleviate the rash. Vinegar can also help neutralise the venom.

CASTAWAY

In severe cases, be prepared to administer cardiopulmonary resuscitation (CPR), instructions for which can be found in Chapter 10.

Urchins can be very painful if you tread on one. Some urchins are venomous and there is a risk of infection. In the first instance, soak your foot in water that's as hot as you can stand, which inactivates the toxins. If you can, apply local antibiotic powder or ointment. The Fijians take ripe papaya (or kiwifruit) and place it on the affected area for about 20–30 minutes. The meat-tenderising enzymes in these fruit will soften the skin so much in that time that the spines can be removed with tweezers or a needle.

Sharks, as you will remember from the movies, will attack humans in a metre (or a little over 3 feet) of water. If you spot a fin, do not shout, splash or kick, but get out of the water as quickly as possible by swimming quietly, using breaststroke. If the shark attacks, punch it in the gills or between the eyes. To avoid encountering one, never swim after dusk, or with an open wound, and never swim where you fish, since your bait may have attracted sharks. Once out of water, hum the theme song from *Jaws*.

7

FLESH, MUST HAVE FLESH!

CASTAWAY

 **[ASTAWAY**

'The killing was the best part. It was the dying I couldn't take.'
    Craig Volk, *Northern Exposure*, 'A-Hunting We Will Go'

A diet of fish can get pretty monotonous, and hunting animals will help vary your diet. More importantly, they will provide you with clothing, glue, bones for tools, gut for cord and many other essentials.

Tracking animals is an art and easiest in snow or on sand because the prints are clear and easy to follow. Rabbit tracks are distinctive because of the combination of long hind and short front feet. Watch an animal moving on muddy ground and then study the footprints it has made. Droppings are a useful sign. You can even identify a seed-eating bird that has found water nearby by its small and mostly liquid droppings.

The best way to attract mammals to a trap is to place salt along a trail or at a water hole. You can also use smoke to drive animals out of their dens or burrows. Snare, club or net the quarry as it emerges. Just don't let Sir Paul McCartney see you doing it.

Trapping animals is easier than hunting them. Traps work in one of four ways: mangle, strangle, dangle, tangle. Deadfalls mangle or crush. Snares strangle. Saplings whip the trap in the air where it dangles. A net tangles.

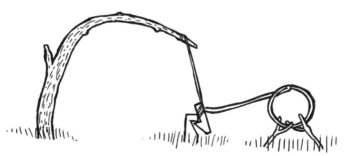
A simple spring snare

Their very name indicates what traps do. They do not always kill their prey, so they are not for the squeamish. The simplest way to catch a small mammal is with a snare. You need a length of springy wire, about 45cm (18 inches) long. Twist a small 'eye' into one end of it and thread the other end through the eye to form a loop that is just large enough for the head of your prey to pass through. Rub earth or animal dung into the wire to mask your smell. Secure the free end to a stake, or tree root, making sure that it will hold firm against any thrashing about, and position the loop carefully in a heavy-traffic area. Funnel the animal into your snare with small twigs pushed into the ground to create barriers. After you have set the trap, sprinkle animal blood or urine in the area to help neutralise your scent.

Set a lot of snares!

A spring snare is more efficient because it whips the animal off the ground, killing it more quickly and keeping it out of reach of other predators. Find a sapling on the edge of a game run strong enough to take the weight of the game. Bend the end of the sapling over and attach it to a notched wooden peg. Hammer another peg into the ground deep enough to make sure it will not be pulled out by the sapling's tension. Next, put your snare wire in the centre of the path and attach another cord (or wire) to the peg securing the sapling. Keep the tension tight. When the animal sticks its head in the snare the tension will dislodge the peg, catapulting the animal into the air. Make sure everything is securely tied, since flying rabbits are hard to find.

Deadfalls are another effective way of killing small game but they do require some careful handling and plenty of practice. Accidentally setting off a Paiute deadfall trap will cause a bruised hand and possibly broken fingers. The principle is the same as the old bucket-of-water-on-teacher trick. When he opens the door the bucket of water empties on his head. A deadfall is triggered when an animal grabs the bait and a large object falls on its head. The weight has to kill the animal, not something you could get away with at school. You do not want to find you have trapped but not killed a wolverine, which is a giant weasel on steroids but much more vicious.

As with the bucket, the trick is getting the deadfall to balance with exactly the right level of precariousness. You want it to go off at exactly the right moment and not when you are setting it up. Most constructions involve sharpened sticks and small branches that counterbalance each other.

The figure-4 trigger can be used for catching desert mice and ground squirrels. The basic trap is constructed from three sticks, notched to form an elongated figure 4. A large rock is propped up by the long diagonal stick with the bait on the lower cross end beneath the rock. The centre stick is pushed into the ground. The sticks are sharpened at the ends and pushed into notches so any movement at the bait end brings the rock down.

A bigger version can be made with heavier logs. Take a forked branch, then sharpen the three ends so it's unstable. Bait the short end. Rest one of the other two ends on a flat rock or piece of wood; the crossbar is then supported by the final end at an angle. Heavy logs and rocks rest on the crossbar, holding the whole edifice precariously in place. When an animal grabs the bait, the whole lot comes crashing down.

Given time and the right tools you can construct some very unpleasant deadfalls using sharpened stakes. However, while Rambo can construct one in thirteen minutes using only his teeth and some dental floss, such sophisticated deadfalls will take days to prepare and often prove more dangerous to their creator than the local wildlife.

For wild pigs, dig a pit on a popular game run leading to a water source. It helps if the ground is soft because the hole is going to have to be at least 1 metre (3.3 feet) square and 1.5 metres (5 feet) deep. Placing sharpened stakes into the bottom will probably not kill the prey but may disable it. Having dug the pit, cover it carefully with branches and foliage that blend in with the run. The covering should be firm enough at the edges so the animal can get right to the middle where everything gives way. Once the pit has been activated, approach it with caution. Make sure the prey is absolutely dead by stabbing it with a spear before hauling it out.

Most birds can be caught in a box trap. A ready-made box, or one made from sticks tied together, is rested with one edge on the ground and the other propped up on a short stick. Tie a length of string round this stick and hide. When the bird wanders underneath the box to investigate the bait, yank the string and the box will trap it.

Bunny boiling

Not being the smartest of creatures, rabbits are relatively easy to catch – especially if they are suffering from myxomatosis, which in its advanced stages renders them blind and unaware of their surroundings. (You can eat rabbits with 'mixi'. The hard part is convincing yourself that something that looks so diseased is edible. Don't eat the liver, which is covered in white spots.) However, an exclusive diet of rabbits can kill you.

In the eighteenth and nineteenth centuries, in the depths of winter up in Hudson Bay, Canada, trappers were discovered dead. They had full bellies but had starved to death. Rabbit flesh is very lean and lacks essential amino acids that our bodies cannot synthesise themselves, but which are crucial for converting food into useable energy. If we eat rabbits and nothing else, our body uses more of those fats and acids in digesting them than it gets in. Replace them or you will will develop the extreme fat hunger known as *rabbit starvation*; in about a week you will develop diarrhoea, with headaches, lassitude and vague discomfort. Death can follow within a few days.

The lesson when boiling bunnies is: don't forget to eat your greens – and fat can be good for you.

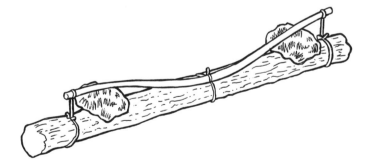

Projectile weapons

Traps are all very well but a real hunter needs a bow. The inventor of the bow and arrow changed the course of history, enabling man to kill game from a distance. Making a bow takes time. As any kid knows, badly made bows lose their power so quickly that the arrow is lucky to clear your toes.

A serious bow comes from wood that's been cut green and left to season for a year. But a serviceable bow can be made in three days. Traditionally, the English long bow was made from yew trees. But any green springy wood (willow, elm, juniper, hazel, oak, ash, birch or hemlock) will do. Select a stave 100–140cm (39.5–55 inches) long, reasonably straight without any major knots and no more than 5cm (2 inches) wide at the centre. Before sawing off the branch, check it for curve. More than one curve on the branch will cause problems.

Find the natural bend by holding both ends of the stave and pushing the middle with your knee. You get more power by working against the natural bend but the bow can twist around when you string it, rendering it useless. Find the centre of the bow using a piece of cord, then mark it with a knife. Next, shape the bow by removing wood from the belly side (the bit facing you when you shoot) with a knife. A vice would be nice; otherwise hold the stave over one knee braced under the other.

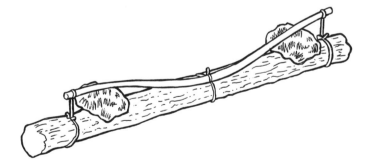

Recurving a bow

The shaped bow, roughly half its original thickness at the handgrip, should taper evenly from the centre and flex evenly. Peel off the bark, since unnecessary cuts on either the belly or backside of the bow will weaken it.

The trick is to recurve the tips to give greater power. Tie the centre of the bow securely to a pole or, preferably, a plank. Then wedge sticks or rocks under the part of the bow where you want the curve. Force the limb down on these sticks and tie it securely. Do not be too rough, since the bow does not have that much strength to bend, and a crack will destroy all your hard work. Now leave to dry for a few days in the sun.

Once it's dry remove it from the frame. If there is a horizontal crack, shave it down beyond the crack and reshape until it flexes evenly. Notch each end of the bow 2.5cm (1 inch) from each end at the sides. Tie the bowstring securely at one end (with a round turn and two half hitches) and make a nonclosing loop at the other so it can be slipped off easily. Release the string when you are not using the bow. The string should be tense but not too tight; the power comes from the drawing-back. Strings can be made from nylon cord, rawhide, homemade cordage or even twisted nettle stems.

Arrow making is called *fletching*. Know anyone called Fletcher? This is what they used to do – or, rather, one of their ancestors. A perfect arrow acts like a coiled spring, releasing energy in flight. Too stiff and it flies like a board. Make them in batches of six at a time. Sod's Law decrees you will lose one and break another, and your prey will run off screaming for its mum with your last arrow embedded in its left buttock.

Arrows should be made from thin straight branches, roughly half the length of the bow (55cm/22 inches long) and about 2cm (0.8 inch) in diameter. Any straight green wood will do – although willow has a tendency to warp and bamboo is too light. Strip off the bark and straighten the arrows by heating the shaft over a hot rock, looking down it or putting it against a piece of tied string. Put aside for a day. If you are using green wood, the arrow will flip out of shape, so perform the process every day for three days. With the wood dry and straight, make a notch about 6mm (0.25 inch) deep and big enough to fit smoothly over the bowstring. It is very embarrassing for the arrow to stay quivering on the string.

Arrows won't fly without being flighted. Traditionally, the best flights are made from goose feathers, though chicken, pigeon, pheasant and, for the flamboyant fletcher, peacock, will all do. If pushed, try paper, light cloth and leaves. Split the feathers from the top to the end of the quill; cut the feather off, leaving about 2cm (0.8 inch) of the quill at each end. Tie the quill ends on to the arrow shaft with thread with the three feathers equally spaced. Make sure you leave 2.5cm (1 inch) of wood clear by the notch. Attach the feathers first with glue if you have any and secure with thread. Or make a two-feather flight by splitting the end of the arrow and pushing in (gently) a complete feather. Make sure it protrudes equally either side.

Wooden arrow tips, sharpened and hardened in the fire, are effective against birds and small game. For larger game, make arrowheads out of shaped and sharpened tin or metal, flint or bone. Bone arrowheads are more resilient than stone and can be made in twenty minutes. Select a bone splinter that is roughly the thickness of the finished point. To shape the point, first abrade the bone flat on any rock with a grainy surface. Rub the tip flat, then shape it into a point and grind the edges into a blade. Don't make it too sharp, as sharp points break off easily. Snap off the arrowhead from the rest of the bone and smooth the end off. To fix it to the arrow, split the end of the arrow, slide in the arrowhead and bind it. Animal sinews are particularly good for this. Applied wet, they dry hard and shrink.

Now's the time to show off your archery skills. Choose your style – Robin Hood or Sioux warrior. The English style is to hold the bow vertical using the index and middle fingers to pull back the arrow into the cheek, where it is sighted and released. Winding a piece of leather around the fingers makes drawing back the string easier. The arrow is rested on the outside of the bow hand with one feather (the cock feather) at right angles to the string, all but resting on your cheek. Native Americans used slightly shorter

bows, holding the bow level or diagonally at stomach level and drawing the string back between thumb and forefinger, aimed and released by feel.

When shooting, wear a long-sleeved shirt buttoned at the cuff or a wrist guard made from a strip of cloth or birch bark on your bow hand. At the moment you release the arrow the string is moving so fast it can flay the skin from your wrist.

If you haven't the time or the tools to make a bow and arrow make an atlatl – a spear thrower. Basically, it's a shaft with a cup at the end in which you place the butt of your spear or dart. The thrower holds the end of the atlatl away from the butt and throws using the upper arm and wrist, getting extra leverage with the snap. Sounds prehistoric? It is.

The atlatl was the precursor of the bow and arrow, its name being derived from the Aztec language Nahuatl. Originally used for fishing, the Aztecs used the atlatl against the Spanish conquistadors, many of whom were fatally surprised when a dart with an obsidian tip passed straight though both sides of their metal armour. A well-made atlatl can send a dart up to 100 metres (109 yards).

To make a simple atlatl, take a tree limb twice the width and a third the length of your dart or spear. The limb should have a fork pointing down but forward; this is your throwing handle. Chisel or gouge out a smooth groove along the upper face so that the dart can travel smoothly. Leave a solid portion at the end to add thrust.

Atlatls are good for fishing, too, as they provide the extra impetus to push the projectile fast through water.

```
┌──────────────────────┐
│  ⌐╖___      CASTAWAY  │
│   ╙─────             │
└──────────────────────┘
```

Using every part of a pig but the squeak: preparing food

For a castaway, nothing should go to waste. When the hunter brings home a kill, you have to act fast.

One for the pot

Let's start by preparing a rabbit for the pot. Avoid initial qualms by not looking at its cute face and banishing all thoughts of *Watership Down* and Disney bunnies from your head. Thinking about Bugs Bunny may in fact make it a lot easier.

Make a cut behind the head into which you can insert two fingers, and then make cuts through the leg joints just above the feet. Make another cut down the middle of the chest from neck to bottom. Do it gently: if you cut into the stomach cavity it will spoil the meat. Pull the skin back from the legs. Once the legs are free, pull down from the neck, removing the fur in one piece. Now cut a line down the belly; give the body a good shake, and the intestines should slide out easily. Scoop out the edible heart, kidneys and liver, and discard the rest, or keep for bait. Chop off the head and wash the body cavity with clean water. Joint the carcass or mount it on a spit.

With larger animals it just takes longer, and it's quite a lot ickier, as there's more blood and more pungent smells. It gets easier, so get on with it. Think of Darwin but don't close your eyes as you're wielding something sharp.

First check the animal is actually dead. Don't be macho. Keep your distance and stab the animal in the neck or its main muscles. If it's still alive the loss of blood will weaken it further, so you can come in and club it with a large rock.

If you are miles from camp and alone with an animal that is too big to carry, you will have to 'field-dress' the body. Hang the carcass by its hind legs and cut the jugular vein or carotid artery in the neck to bleed it out. This prevents the meat from spoiling and is essential if you have caught a pig.

Whenever possible, let the blood drain into a container placed under the head. Blood is packed full of the nutrients, vitamins, minerals and salt that you need to keep healthy. Don't drink the blood fresh unless you hail from Transylvania, but cook thoroughly. Blood adds flavour and thickens stews and soups. The Masai of East Africa eat no fruit or grain but one of their diet staples is cow's milk mixed with blood.

The longer an animal is dead the more the stomach bloats. The bacteria continue to process the animal's last meal but the animal can't fart to relieve the pressure. Gutting as soon as possible prevents bloating and cools the carcass, which assists in preserving the meat. The hotter the weather, the faster meat spoils. Removing the innards will also reduce the weight of the animal, making it easier to carry back to camp.

Hang the body or place on a slight incline, head uphill. Make a cut upwards from the anus, being careful not to rupture the intestinal wall. Next, cut through the fat and meat on the belly. Using a knife and mallet to cut through the pelvic bone of a deer where the two halves join helps remove the intestines. Cut through the breastbone to open up the chest cavity.

The whole body is now opened up, so make a small cut across the throat to release the oesophagus, take hold if it and roll the intestines out of the body cavity. Keep the kidneys, liver, heart and the fat surrounding the intestines. All are delicious. Tongues, brains and eyes are all edible. Guts can be used for all sorts of things: cleaned-out intestine makes sausage skin; bladders are an effective water bag; you can fill the stomach lining with water and boil it by lobbing in hot rocks. Deer bones make effective tools and the tendons can be used for sinew fibres.

Skinning and butchering a deer

Some people might prefer to remove the skin first before gutting a deer but that increases the risk of spoiling the meat. (If you have a wild pig, do not skin it at all: gut it, then place the carcass in embers and scrape the singed hair off.)

Make a cut around the neck and use the knife blade to work the hide above the front shoulders. Bend the legs until you can see the joints, and cut through them. Next, split the skin open along the inside of the legs. Put down the knife to avoid making unnecessary holes, grab the hide by the neck and peel down using your body weight to apply an even pressure. It comes away surprisingly easily. Cut around the tail and, hey presto, one skin is ready to be flayed and turned into nice warm clothes and accessories.

Generally, back legs produce a tastier cut – rump, fillet and leg joints – while the front legs can be stringier and need slow cooking. Forget fancy cuts unless Gordon Ramsay is part of your group. If he is, get him to do the bloody bits.

Start by quartering the animal. Split it down the backbone, then count down the ribs and cut between the tenth and eleventh. Cut into smaller, manageable chunks. Flex the limbs to find the ball joints, then cut through them. To remove all the meat from a deer or sheep, you will need a meat saw. If you don't have one use your knife. Chuck the bones into boiling water to make a stock. When removing steaks, cut *across* the muscles rather than with them. The meat along both sides of the backbone is very tender and can be peeled off easily. Removing meat from bones often leaves small strips of meat, which can be thrown into stews or dried.

Eat the offal first – liver, kidneys, heart – since it goes off faster. Hanging tenderises meat and kills any lingering parasites. Butchers are always boasting about how they hang their Aberdeen Angus beef for 28 days. Pheasants and other game birds are often hung, ungutted, for several days, as this improves the flavour. Allegedly. So hang the bigger cuts of meat in a cool place for a few days before slicing off a tender steak. If it's boiling hot, cook, salt or dry your meat immediately.

Keep eating the rocks ...

... otherwise you could be in trouble. Edible salt (sodium chloride) is an essential mineral, one of very few rocks commonly eaten – and enjoyed – by humans. Your body loses salt when you sweat and when you pee and must be replaced.

Salt is an ever-present ingredient of the prepackaged, manufactured mush that passes for food in the UK, so it is very easy to consume more than the 10 grams our bodies require every day. Too much salt can lead to long-term health problems such as high blood pressure. Too little salt leads to dizziness, nausea, lethargy, tiredness and unexplained muscle cramps. (Ever woken up in the middle of the night with your calf locked and raked by jabbing red-hot needles of pain that rattle the teeth? That could be caused by a salt deficiency due to exercise – or a mega-hangover caused by dehydration.) A craving for salt can also mean that your body requires other trace minerals.

If you feel as if you're not getting enough salt, drink a pint of water with a pinch of salt in it. Taking a long cool drink of seawater will result in projectile vomiting. Adding fresh water to dilute it will be much kinder and effective for your body. Away from the coast, boiling the roots of certain trees (hickory, the nipa palm) dry will leave black salt crystals. Animal blood is packed full of essential minerals.

Salt makes food taste nicer and its value has been recognised throughout history. The Phoenicians built an economic empire by making and selling salt; in ancient Rome wages were paid in salt (hence the word *salary*); while in medieval times Malian merchants in Timbuktu valued salt higher than gold.

The Phoenicians harvested salt by flooding land with seawater, then leaving it to dry. Using solar heat and wind is still the easiest way to make salt. Find a rock pool that has been created by a high tide or storm. Evaporation will have left salt traces around the edges. Don't worry about the colour – salt comes white, pale pink or light grey. Scrape these traces up (a credit card could come in handy), trying not to get many barnacles or rock flakes. Boiling seawater in large cans will speed up the evaporation process. Salt is essential in helping to preserve food.

Preserving food

Nature's freezer
In Little Diomede, Alaska, the local Inupiaq Inuit kill walrus in the spring, dig a meat hole 2.5 metres (8 feet) down in the tundra, cover it and plant a marker so they can recognise their hole. In the autumn, they dig it up and eat it a piece at a time. The hole keeps the meat chilled but also breaks it down so it tastes like a particularly pungent cheese. It is an acquired taste and requires a natural freezer.

Drying food
Lightweight, compact and nutritious, if not always delicious, dried food is an essential survival food if you are trekking across country. It can be chewed or put into water, soups and stews to rehydrate.

Nearly any type of meat can be made into jerky or biltong as long as it is parasite-free. Trim off any fat, skin and tendons, bone it and cut into thin strips. The thinner they are the easier they are to dry and digest later. Soak in brine (100g/3.5 ounces of salt to 1 litre/1.75 pints of water) for 24 hours, then rinse and dry. Hang the strips 2–3 metres (6.5–10 feet) above the ground in direct sunlight where there is a good airflow. Keep turning the meat and keep flies off – the drying process could take up to two weeks. If you have string to spare you can thread it through the top of the meat using a needle or bamboo sliver. Meat is ready for storage when it is completely dry and flexible but brittle enough to break when it is bent in half.

Drying fish is a much quicker process using hot sun-baked rocks. Gut, cut off the head, tail and any protruding fins, remove the backbone, then make diagonal scores in the flesh. Place on a rock.

To dry fruit and vegetables wash them, peel if you wish – though this removes nutrients – and slice thinly. Spread in a single layer, with pieces not touching, on drying trays and turn daily. Window frames and door frames make good drying trays. To intensify the heat, an old piece of glass can be placed several centimetres above the food. Set the tray on rocks or pieces of wood to allow air circulation.

The process of drying food works only if you ensure it's entirely moisture-free. It needs to be stored in a dry place in an airtight container. One mouldy piece will spoil all the others it is stored with. It is easier to dry food in a desert, where there is low humidity. Trying to dry food in a tropical rainforest is akin to wrestling sand. It's not going to happen. Ever.

If it's humid you need to force-dry or smoke your meat over a fire. Since a fancy smokehouse is unavailable, build your own smoking tepee. Find three straight branches, about 5cm (2 inches) thick at the base and cut to the same size. Bind them at the top to create a firm tripod. Cut a notch on the outside of each leg 40cm (15.5 inches) from the base. Make a lattice platform from pliable branches and secure this on to the legs

Make a fire, gathering a pile of green leaves (no grass, nothing flammable or toxic) preferably from hardwood trees. Prepare the meat and fish as for drying. If smoking space is at a premium, gut the fish first. Then run a cord through the gills under the head and tie to the tripod.

When the flames have died down pile the leaves over the embers. Cover the tepee with a damp cloth, or leafy boughs, bark strips and turf, to keep in the smoke. Smoking will take 18 hours but keep an eye on the tepee. If it's sending out enough smoke signals for a powwow, cover it some more.

Pickling and salting

Ceviche – raw fish covered in lemon or lime juice – is found all over Latin America. Preserved lemons are a staple of North African cooking. To pickle meat or fish, add two parts citric acid to one part water, and marinate the flesh for over twelve hours. Store in an airtight container with liquid covering the meat. Vegetables can be cooked and then preserved in brine. The solution should be so salty that a potato will bob around on the surface.

If you have large airtight container and loads of salt, consider salting meat. Salt draws out moisture and creates an inhospitable environment for bacteria. Two great maritime empires, Portugal and Great Britain, relied on bacalhau and salt pork to preserve food on board ship. Bacalhau is salted cod, sun-dried into stiff slabs that keep for months and are then soaked in cool water before cooking.

Meat salted in cold weather (so that it has no chance to spoil while the salt takes effect) can last for years. John Steinbeck's *The Grapes of Wrath* describes the process of filling a wooden barrel with salt and meat:

> *Noah carried the slabs of meat into the kitchen and cut it into small salting blocks, and Ma patted the course salt in, laid it piece by piece in the kegs, careful that no two pieces touched each other. She laid the slabs like bricks, and pounded salt in the spaces.*

Salting was around long before fridge-freezers. When it's time to eat the meat, simply wash the salt off and cook. When opening an airtight container, make sure you re-cover the contents with salt. Otherwise the meat will spoil, and so will you.

SHIT HAPPENS! Phobia Corner 1

Even Indiana Jones had a problem with **snakes**. To help keep you
and the serpents apart, never swim in muddy water, but do wear
stout boots and watch where you step. Use a stick to turn over rocks
or dig around under logs. Check your bedding and packs every night.
Many snakes live in trees, so be careful when picking fruit.

There are no general rules about how to identify whether a snake
is venomous, so play it safe. If you see a snake, back away slowly.
Snakes can strike half their body length away and some are around
a couple of metres (6 feet or so) long. Keep calm – the snake is
probably even more intent on escape than you are. Only a few snakes
are reported to have aggressively attacked man – the king cobra,
the bushmaster and tropical rattlesnake of South America, and the
mamba of Africa – but even these creatures do so only occasionally.

Fortunately, few snake bites are fatal if the patient is given the
correct antivenin within a few hours. Even if you don't have it, don't
panic. Few snakes actually kill with one bite. Remain calm and don't
move about, as this hastens the passage of the poison around
your body. Keep the bitten area lower than the heart. Wash the bite
to remove any venom still on the surface and place a restricting
bandage above the bite. Place the wound in cold water or ice if
available to get it as cool as possible. Be ready to administer artificial
respiration. Never try to suck out the poison – that's stuff for movies
only. If it was a spitter you encountered, this is dangerous only if it
lands in the eyes or an open cut. Wash out immediately. If bitten, try
to remember what the snake looked like, or, even better, kill it. There
are different antidotes for different types of snake venom.

The good news is that there are no poisonous snakes at all in Ireland,
Jamaica, Haiti, Cuba, Polynesia and New Zealand.

8

LORDING IT

CASTAWAY

CASTAWAY

'We act as though comfort and luxury were the chief requirements of life, when all that we need to make us happy is something to be enthusiastic about.'

Charles Kingsley (1819-75)

Go on, have a feast. It's good for the soul and great for the stomach. Just because you're a castaway, it doesn't mean you can't throw a party to welcome the new moon, celebrate catching a wild pig or making a piece of cord more than a foot long that doesn't break when you use it. Sometimes it's important to savour delicious food rather than wolf down lumps of fuel.

Castaway parties do need a lot of preparation so, instead of sending out embossed 'At Cave' invitations, start digging a large hole to make a steam pit.

You'll find steam-pit cooking all over the Pacific. The New Zealand Maori call it a *hangi*, in Peru it's a *pachamanca*, in Hawaii they cook *kalua* in an *imu*, while the Chileans call the dish *curanto*. Over in New England it's a *clambake*. The principle is the same. Dig hole, chuck red hot rocks in hole, put in food, cover with herbs and earth. Leave to steam for hours. Yum.

OK, there's a little more to it than that and it's a lot of effort to cook one seagull, a handful of mussels and some root vegetables your mate swears are related to the potato family. In order to eat as dusk falls you need to start first thing in the morning.

Back to the hole. The pit needs to be roughly three times bigger than the amount of food you intend to cook. So, if you are cooking a Hawaiian salt pig, that is one big hole: 1.8 metres (6 feet) by 1.2 metres (4 feet) by 0.9 metres (3 feet) deep! For a single chicken it might be 45cm (18 inches) in diameter but about 30cm (1 foot) deep. Reserve the dirt that you have dug out.

Line the floor and the sides of the pit with flat stones. Dense lava rocks and basalt are best; granite can explode under the great heat of the fire; if in

doubt, choose heavy smooth rocks. Next, build a fire the entire length of your pit. Let it burn for at least ninety minutes.

While the fire is blazing away, gather a lot of fibrous plant material. Now gather some more. Grass is OK but if you can find something with flavour – seaweed (if you're serving seafood), banana fig or white cabbage leaves – then use that. It has got to be fibrous. The greener the better. Soak dried grass in water. Non-fibrous leaves may wilt down, exposing the food to the heat source, where it will char badly.

Once the rocks are glowing red hot, remove any unburned wood and scrape out the remaining coals. Add a layer of greens 20–30cm (8–12 inches) thick. If they have been soaking in water, there will be a satisfying whoosh of steam. Now place your food on the greens. Cover the food with another thick layer of greens. Add the oven roof: a layer of bark slabs, wood slats or a large rock. This should create enough of a barrier between the food and the dirt you are going to cover it with. Nobody likes lobster with an earth garnish.

Cover the pit completely with dirt. If you see steam or smoke escaping from around the edges of the pit cover it with more bark and even more dirt. If any air gets in, the food will burn and your meal will be destroyed. Once the pit is sealed, your food will keep cooking, but it will never burn. In *hangis* the food is often protected by a layer of cloth, or cold sacks, while clambakers prefer a canvas soaked in seawater.

Now leave the pit and go and do something useful for at least three hours. Even a half-kilo (1-pound) fish will take at least an hour, and the bigger the piece of meat, the longer it needs to steam. Forget the thirty-minutes-per-kilo rule for meat you use at home and be prepared to wait as long as five to six hours for larger pieces of meat. After all that effort, don't risk undercooking your meal.

When it's time, be careful removing the dirt. Scrape and brush aside as much as you can and then carefully remove the bark covering with the earth.

You can cook anything in a steam pit, from guinea pigs to whole lambs, sweet potato, shellfish, red mullet and mackerel. The steaming moistens rather than dries out the food. The longer a tough old game bird cooks, the more tender the meat becomes – and it tastes great.

Making hide and furs

Clothes eventually wear out. Living rough speeds up this process and with the nearest Marks & Spencer out of reach you may have to start making your own. Prepare early for the arrival of winter, when nighttime temperatures plummet.

Wearing fur is one option. In Siberia, where minus 20ºC is T-shirt weather, fur hats and coats are essential. They provide layers of insulation but they also breathe, so you don't internally combust from heat exhaustion. A fur coat is more manoeuvrable than a duvet with arms.

Your choice of whether to keep the fur on or off will depend on what the uses are and the animal skin you have. Deer have short bristly hair rather than fur, so you should turn their hide into buckskin shirts, moccasins and water bags. Rabbit furs sewn together make for a very warm coat or bed covering. Sheepskins make great coats and rugs.

The first step is fleshing the hide, removing any meat, membrane and fat left on after the skinning. Peg the hide on to a flat rock, then scrape it using a blunt knife, flint or hard plastic. Take care not to cut into the skin. It should not take more than half an hour to flesh a deer hide. If you have several hides, leave them out for ants and insects to help remove the flesh.

To make buckskin you must dehair the skin completely and remove every layer of the epidermis. Soak the hide in water for two to four days. The water eats away at the follicles and when you can yank a clump of hairs out of the neck you're ready. This is harder to do than removing the membrane from the underside of the skin. Attach the skin securely to a tree and then

scrape down from the neck following the hairs. Put some effort in, as it will take two to three hours of hard work to dehair a deer.

To cure the hide, lay it out flat to dry in the sun. Stretch it out so that it is all exposed to the air. Get rid of folds, because they will stay damp and rot. If there is no sunshine, rub the skin with ash or salt and force-dry it over a fire (don't do this anywhere near cooking food, as steam will dampen it down again). To store a hide, lay it flat in a dry place. A properly stored hide will keep for months until you are ready to start brain tanning.

Brain tanning? An old adage claims, 'Every animal has enough brains to tan its own hide' – another reason for scooping out the brains of your kill. The brain contains lecithin, an oil that lubricates the hide, enabling you to stretch it until it is soft and pliable. Make sure your hands are free of cuts, as brain matter can give you a nasty infection. Cooking the brains in a little water sterilises them, reducing this risk. Mash the brains up with your clean unscratched paws. Stop shuddering, it's really good for the skin!

Put cooked, mashed brains in a large container and add warm water (3–4 litres/5–7 pints if skin is dried out, less if it's damp). Warm water thins the lecithin so it penetrates the hide more easily; boiling water will shred it into useless rags. Leave the hide in the brain water overnight. When you fish it out, the skin side should have gone deathly white. Wring out the brain matter and then stretch the hide as far as you can until it is dry and soft to touch. This can take up to 24 hours. If it dries out stiff as a board then you have to repeat the braining, soaking and stretching process.

Glue

This can be made from animal skins, tendons, hooves, cartilage, membranes, horns, antlers and fish skins – all the leftover stuff you were going to chuck. If you're using a whole hide, dehair it first. Cut the hide into small scraps a centimetre (0.5 inch) square, put a large handful in a full can of water and cook it all day. Do not boil, since this weakens the glue.

The hide dissolves slowly in hot water, becoming thicker and darker as the water evaporates. Adding more scraps and simmering the water away makes it thicker.

Making glue is a pungent process. It has to be used warm because heating extracts both gelatine and glue from the hide and once it cools it sets like jelly. It rots after a few days, but will keep indefinitely when dried out, frozen or kept simmering. Store the flakes or small blocks in a dry place and then add to water when you need to stick things together. Could come in very handy.

Champagne moments

What are you missing most from your old life? Is it your family, friends, much-loved places? Or is it – perish the thought! – fags and booze?

To help with nicotine cravings, try drying and then rolling some dulse seaweed, and then using it as chewing tobacco. If it is a drink you're after, then there are a whole range of possibilities. Do remember, though, what happened to the Pitcairn mutineers when they worked out how to distil alcohol from the root of the cabbage tree. It made Saturday night in Norwich seem tame in comparison.

Enough of the party pooping. Let's get hammered.

Your building blocks are water, sugar, fruit and yeast (but not necessarily all of them), some containers and a lot of patience. Sugar is easier to find than you'd think. As well as looking for cane and honey, check plants for the thick roots that often contain fructose. The cabbage tree stem has more of this than sugar beet. Yeast can be homemade by boiling up hops or potatoes in water (the flower of a coconut tree is just as good), and then combining the liquid with sugar, salt and flour, or flour substitute. Let sit for two days in a sealed container, then it's ready. (You could, of course, even use it for making bread!)

For your basic 'champagne' just mix some type of sugar, water and yeast. The yeast eats sugar in the water environment, producing alcohol and carbon dioxide. To this you can add pretty much any crazy stuff you want – try spices, fruit and grains. The water could, of course, be fruit juice or coconut milk. Bottle it with a porous lid. Let it sit for a week, then stop the yeast's action by immersing the bottle in the coldest water you can find. Then you're away – it might be brutal on the taste buds, but it will be lethal on the senses.

It can be even simpler. Out of the bud of the coconut tree's flower is a juice called coconut toddy or *tuba*. Coconut milk left for five days will ferment by itself. Some then distil the toddy, producing an alcoholic spirit known locally as *lambanog*, which is 98 per cent proof.

Grape juice will ferment into wine; alternatively dry your grapes and add the raisins to boiling water with sugar and, ideally, lemon. Stir daily for six days. Strain, bottle and keep in a cool place for ten days, and your raisin wine is ready.

What you get will depend on its storage, what type of sugar is used, how pure the water is and the type of yeast used. And whatever else you added to the mixture.

Not a wine man myself

The idea of a beer may have been preying on your mind. Unless you have malt, or the means to prepare it, abandon this idea. Don't despair, however, since you can make mead, in which the sugar in question is honey.

Mead is the classic drink (yes, it came before beer) of fermented honey, producing a fine honey 'wine'. This was the drink of the Vikings, the 'ambrosia' of the Greek gods. Add fruits, grains or nutmeg to honey, ferment it, and you produce a wide array of other mead-ish drinks with their own unique taste. You need grape juice (concentrated by heating), honey and water.

And a lot of time. The bee stings you suffered getting the damn honey will be long healed by the time you taste your mead. You must let it ferment uncovered for three months, then bottle it. After six months you will find a bitter, and frankly pretty nasty mess. If you leave it for a year you may have a brew that is smooth and sparkly. Leave it for two and a half years, and you could well have a crisp and subtly sweet taste, with bubbles like champagne.

Making a sundial

If you need to know when cocktail hour starts, make a sundial. Push a tall stick into the ground. Mark the end of the stick's shadow when the sun rises in the morning and again at evening just before it sets. Draw a semicircle around the stick that connects the first and last points and mark the midpoint (midday). You now have a dial to keep track of time.

Perchance to dream: making your bed and lying in it

Hot beds

It may be that your idea of luxury is more a warm dry bed than night down the pub. In that case, why not treat yourself to a hot-coal bed? Dig a trench 20cm (8 inches) deep, up to 30cm (12 inches) wide and the length of your body. Build a fire and let it burn very hot for two to three hours in the entire trench. When the fire starts to die down, remove any unburned lumps of wood, then cover the coals with dirt. Check that there aren't any hot spots. If there are, put on more earth.

You do need a tarpaulin or poncho to place on top of the earth before you go to bed. Otherwise the steam that the heat of the fire generates from the moisture in the soil will have you soggy and miserable by morning.

An A-frame tube bed

Actually, this is more of a necessity than a luxury – do not underestimate the importance of quality rest and sleep.

Drive two pairs of sturdy sticks into the ground at an angle, leaving a distance of slightly more than your height between the pairs.

Tie the top of each pair together to create an A-frame. Make a tube of strong material (a salvaged sail, plastic sacking or a groundsheet is ideal) sewn or pinned together. Choose two strong, straight poles, slightly longer than the distance between the two A-frames, and pass them through the tube of material.

Place the sticks over the frames so that they rest on the sides with the tube preventing them from slipping any lower.

Without strong material, you will have to tie the poles securely to the A-frames and lay branches across the two poles. Then cover this platform with softer bedding such as grass, moss or leaves. This bedding does require frequent changing. If the ground is too hard to drive in the feet, you will need to tie cross-members between the two frames.

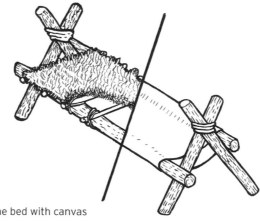

The perfect A-frame bed with canvas or grass mattress

SHIT HAPPENS! Phobia Corner 2

Only 27 of 35,000 species of **spider** have been known to kill a human. Most deadly spiders are dark and patterned with yellow, white or red spots. **Black widows** are small and dark, with thin legs and a distinctive red, yellow or white marking on the abdomen, often in the shape of an hourglass. Bites from these produce severe pain, cramps, shivering and sweating, and weakness that can knock you out for a week. They are rarely fatal, however, unlike the most dangerous spider in the world. The Australian **funnelweb** is grey or dark brown with small chunky legs, an aggressive nature and a bite that can kill within fifteen minutes. Treat the patient as if they were bitten by a snake, keeping the body still to avoid aiding the circulation of the venom.

Tarantulas – very large and hairy, these might be everyone's spider nightmare, but their bites, while painful, are not disabling. New Zealand has been spared the funnelweb, but has a brother, the **tunnelweb**, which sets traps of silk on the undersides of stones or logs. Its bite is painful, as the spider has very large fangs, but no more dangerous than a bee sting. On New Zealand beaches, you will also find the **false katipo**, a small black spider with a painful, though not dangerous, bite. **White-tailed** spiders are also common, on the walls of houses and in cool damp spots. Their bites cause pain, nausea and swelling at the bite site and some flu-like symptoms. The bite can develop into a small ulcerous wound that heals inside a week.

Spider bites should always be cleaned and watched for signs of infection, a much more common cause of problems than venom. A cold compress can help reduce the considerable pain.

And finally – **scorpions**. Do not panic, Mr Bond. While the 1,100 species of scorpion can all sting, only twenty possess venom of sufficient toxicity to kill. In North Africa and the Middle East, do beware the **deathstalker** and the **fat-tailed scorpion**. But, because it takes several days to replenish their poison supply, they seldom deliver enough to kill. Scorpion stings usually produce only pain, numbness or swelling. That said, in scorpion zones, check your boots in the morning and your bedding at night.

9

DIRE
STRAITS

CASTAWAY

Shit happens.

Just when everything is going so well, life has a habit of taking an unexpected detour and dumping you in the excrement. A castaway is at the mercy of nature and, while statistically rare, erupting volcanoes, tsunamis, hurricanes, cyclones, tornadoes and earthquakes do happen. Fierce storms and high winds are almost inevitable. The consequences can be serious, destroying your campsite and your possessions, taking you back to the early days on the island – but worse.

Natural disasters

Hurricanes

Hurricanes come by different names – typhoons in the China Sea, cyclones in the Indian Ocean and willy-willy in northwest Australia. Stop sniggering. Winds of over 200 m.p.h. (320 k.p.h.) – beyond Force 12 on the Beaufort Scale – are nothing to laugh about.

The first signs are rooster tails – long, thin clouds – curving up from the horizon. These grow more and more numerous until they cover the sky. Black clouds begin moving overhead. Above the horizon the hurricane can be seen rising dirty white, turning grey, and then black. Winds become stronger and stronger, filling the air with salty mist as the ocean waves crash with increasing power. The entire sky turns black and lightning flashes.

If the hurricane hits the island full on it will demolish any temporary structure (bye-bye, wigwam) and strip the roof off many a house. Unless your dwelling has a solid cellar your best bet is to retreat to a cave, taking essential tools, supplies and lots of water. If you're caught in the open, dive into a ditch, lie flat on the ground and crawl into the leeside of any solid rocky outcrop or, as a last resort, a line of large trees (a 'last resort' because the high winds can uproot trees).

After some hours the winds slow down, the howling replaced by an eerie calm. You're in the eye of the hurricane and you have less than an hour before the winds start again – from the opposite direction. If you're outside, try to find a better shelter; if you can't, get around the other side of the rocks and batten down for another buffeting.

Tornadoes

Tornadoes, or twisters, can happen anywhere in the world – the UK has the world's highest number of reported tornadoes for its land area. On 7 December 2006, a tornado ripped through Kensal Rise in north London, injuring six people, removing roofs and, in all, damaging 150 houses. It lasted ten seconds.

Tornadoes are created by warm and cold winds travelling at different speeds and in different directions, often on the back of a thunderstorm, creating a build-up of energy as in a pressure cooker. The weather fronts come together to create a violent twisting vortex 25–60 metres (27–65 yards) across that drags along the ground at speeds of up to 400 m.p.h. (645 k.p.h.), sucking everything it can up into the air. The huge cloud, called a *supercell*, also generates ferocious lightning and hail.

Signs that a twister is coming include the sky turning dark with a green hue. Low-hanging clouds look like a dark wall in the sky. Because tornadoes can occur near the back end of a thunderstorm, you may be deceived by the clear, sunlit skies behind it, and the funnel shape may be hidden by heavy rain. But, as it gathers pace, the tornado roars like an angry jet plane and its arrival is often heralded by giant hailstones and a cloud of debris.

As in a hurricane, the safest place to shelter is a storm cellar or a cave. Keep well away from windows. Close the shutters or windows facing the twister and open those on the other side – this equalises the pressure and should stop the twister taking your roof with it. In the open you are in danger of being hit by flying debris or picked up by the winds.

[ASTAWAY

However, you can usually see it coming, so get out of the way by running at a right angle to its path. Take shelter in a ditch, lie flat and start praying the twister isn't aiming to catch you.

Earthquakes/tsunamis

Nature does provide a few early-warning signs. A few months before an earthquake hits, the average temperature of the area keeps increasing. The day of the earthquake it is a whopping 5–9ºC (41–48ºF) above the average seasonal norm. Any sudden change in water flow – the stream slows to a trickle or comes down in torrents – can also indicate an earthquake is coming in a few days. The water level in wells may rise or fall by as much as a metre (3.3 feet) while the water may turn muddy or a fountain appear in the ground.

Ten to twenty-hours before an earthquake, the entire animal kingdom becomes highly disturbed, restless and fearful. Birds do not sit on trees but move about at a low height, emitting a shrill noise. Rodents panic while domesticated animals struggle against being penned in or tied up, and can even turn on their owners.

Humans, too, know something is up. Hospitals report that some patients become highly disturbed, exhibiting a sudden rise in blood pressure, heart trouble, headache, migraine and respiratory disorders. Psychosomatic disorders and the number of patients visiting the casualty departments increase by up to seven times in the day before the quake.

To survive an earthquake, move fast. Time is of the essence. Put out the fire and head for the cellar if you have one. If caught outside, do not try to run, as you will be thrown about by the shifting earth and possibly swallowed by a fissure in the ground – just as in the movies. Keep away from anything tall and potentially unstable (trees, cliffs). Caves are not a good idea in this instance, as a rock fall could block your exit. If you're up a hill, get up to the top, cutting down the chances of being caught by a rockslide. Provided it's not overshadowed by a cliff, the beach is safe but only during the quake itself. Once it stops, run for the high ground in case there is a tsunami coming.

A tidal wave can hit without your feeling a quake beforehand. The surf sounds different. The water recedes as if the tide had pulled out in a hurry, exposing the seafloor and stranding fish – yes, it's that quick. The water stays low for several minutes. Then the sea rises, as quickly and quietly as it disappeared, but it keeps on rising, higher than the high tide mark. Then comes the first tidal wave. They can reach 30 metres (nearly 100 feet) high and there will be more than one.

If your camp is close to the sea and something breaks the normal pattern, don't take the opportunity to go gather a gasping grouper. Get everybody off the beach, grab as many essentials as you can put into a pack or a bag and head for the nearest high ground. Give yourself no more than two minutes. Sure, it might be a false alarm. But it also might destroy your home and take your life. Return when the sea has been acting normally for at least two tides.

Don't feel a fool. Better a cautious castaway than a dead one.

🪢 Emergency water collection

In the aftermath of disaster water supplies can be disrupted and polluted. Don't worry: there are plenty of ways to get enough water.

Place a polythene sheet over a small bush, creating a plastic tent. Dig channels at the bottom of the tent and line them with plastic. Suspend the top of the tent above the bush with string or a padded stick. Make sure that no leaves are touching the sides, and the water vapour that is released by the bush will then drip down into your little water tanks.

Rainwater is clean and easy to collect. Leave receptacles out in a clearing. After it rains you will have a nice cool drink waiting. Even if it doesn't rain at night, dawn brings the dew. Use a piece of clean cloth to wipe dew from foliage and then wring it out into a cup. You can also tie the cloths around your legs and ankles and walk through wet vegetation. Then either suck the

CASTAWAY

cloths dry or wring them out. If you suspect a plant to be poisonous don't gather dew from it; if possible, boil dew water.

Solar stills are particularly effective in climates where it is hot by day and cold at night. Over 24 hours the still should collect up to 550ml (1 pint) of water and it is a very effective way of distilling drinkable water out of urine, sea and polluted water. Site the still in the dampest place you can find – a dry river bed, clay soil, or where there is already vegetation. It must be in the full sun to work.

Dig a hole about 90cm (35 inches) across and 45cm (18 inches) down – deep enough to place a can or other water receptacle in. Take a plastic sheet, tarpaulin or space blanket and roughen the underside with a stone. Clear plastic is better than opaque, since it absorbs less heat. Secure the sheet over the hole by weighing it down with rocks or logs, and put a small rock in the middle, directly above your water container. During the daytime heat raises the temperature of the air and the earth underneath the sheet, producing vapour. This condenses on the underside of the plastic, where it will collect and drip into your water container. You may also find that the still becomes a live larder if snakes or small animals get stuck under the plastic.

To distil, boil seawater in a covered pot and run a tube under the cover of the solar still. Cover any joins with mud or sand to prevent the steam from escaping. Bear in mind that distilling seawater takes a long time and requires a lot of fuel.

You can also make a solar still for use at sea with a bucket and some plastic. Place a cup in the centre of the bottom of the bucket. Saturate some cloth with seawater and wrap it around the cup. Alternatively add to the bottom of the bucket any plant material or spare liquids, such as urine or blood. Stretch a piece of plastic over the bucket, with a weight in the centre over the cup. Tie the plastic around the rim of the bucket. To improve efficiency and speed of condensation put cold seawater on top.

If you have some flexible plastic tubing, tie one end inside the water cup and the other end outside the bucket. If you take the still apart to get the water out it will take an hour or so for the air to resaturate.

A working solar still for use at sea

Never drink seawater or urine unless it is distilled! It takes twice as much water for your body to process seawater as you get from it. If you drink salt water, you will probably pee yourself to death and die of dehydration more quickly than if you hadn't drunk anything at all. The body needs to get rid of all the sodium in the salt, so it increases urination, stealing fluids from other parts of the body. Urine is full of substances your body wants to get rid of. It you put it back in, your body will try to get rid of it as quickly as possible. Don't do it.

Food for the desperate

Seals are actually the best food source in the Arctic, and their blubber can be used for fuel and their skins for shoes. To catch them, wait by an air hole in the ice, and hit them with a stick when they come up to breathe. Watch out for polar bears.

CASTAWAY

Snakes and **lizards** are good to eat. Cut off their heads and gut them. With snakes take off at least another 8cm (3 inches) to remove all poison glands. The skin will peel off easily once you have slit its underside. Remove the gut and then wash the flesh and either stew it or wrap it in grass or damp leaves and cook it in mud. This one does taste like chicken.

Small rodents are edible. Cut off the feet and gut and skin them. Pound the remainder, including the head, until the bones are ground up enough to eat. Boil them. Skinning mice is a fiddly process, and there isn't much meat on them, anyway. Better to roast them whole in the embers. The fire burns off the fur and the bones are so small they crunch up easily. Think of them as sardines in a fur coat.

Skin **frogs** and **toads** before cooking, as the skins of many species secrete irritating and poisonous fluids. (Licking toads may lead to hallucinations!) Avoid those marked yellow or red. Find them at night by their croaking. Approach slowly, then club them with a stick or snag the larger ones with a hook and line. Kill them by sticking a knife through the spinal cord just behind the head. Doesn't taste of chicken.

Emergency plants

Think of **dandelions** as beneficial herbs not a weed. The greens (and roots of young plants) can be used in salads, as a cooked vegetable, and made into tea. The flowers may be better dipped and fried. The blossoms can make a nonalcoholic drink. Boiling dandelion or dock leaves, changing the water halfway through, helps to remove their bitterness.

Sea rocket, which grows on dunes, is part of the mustard family and, while hardly delicious, serves as a famine food. Leaves, stems, flower buds and immature seedpods can be eaten raw or cooked; although rich in vitamin C, they have a very bitter taste. Roots dried and ground into a powder, then mixed with cereal flours can be used to make bread.

While not the first thing that occurs to you when hungry, on the islands off New Zealand **bracken** (rarauhe – the fern, aruhe – the edible rhizome) was a staple of the Maori diet since it grew all year round and was not seasonal although it had to be set on fire to produce pollen for regrowth. Its root is 60 per cent white starch that can be eaten raw, cooked or dried and ground into a powder, which can be stored for years. The larger fronds have an unbearably disgusting taste, but young shoots can be eaten raw for the best nutritional value or cooked by blanching them in boiling water and soaking in cold water for a couple of hours. In Japan they are a delicacy.

Bracken also has many medicinal uses. A poultice of the pounded fronds and leaves was used by the Maori to treat sores, and the leaves were used in a steam bath as a treatment for arthritis. A tea made from the roots treated stomach cramps, chest pains, internal bleeding, diarrhoea and colds, and also was used to expel worms.

A glue can be made from the rootstock. The fibrous remnants from edible roots make a good tinder. The rhizome lathers readily in water and can be used as a soap. Root extract has been used as a hair wash and rubbed into the scalp to promote hair growth. The roots can be pounded to remove the bark, split into flat bands and used to weave baskets. The dried ferns produce a very durable thatch. The leaves, which repel insects, are used as a packing material for fruit, a lining for baskets, fruit-drying racks and bedding. All in all, quite useful.

CASTAWAY

Last night a turtle saved my life

In 1540 Pedro de Serrano was the only survivor of a shipwreck in the Pacific. The Spaniard was plunged into the sea wearing only his shirt and belt and carrying just a knife. He managed to swim to an island and dragged himself on to the shore. But the island had no vegetation, no shade and no wood to build a fire and shelter. Worst of all, there was no fresh water, only sand that reflected the burning sun and quickly absorbed any rain that fell during the brief but ferocious storms.

After resting, de Serrano awoke determined to stay alive. He found cockles and shrimps along the beach, which he ate raw. But his biggest problem was thirst. Here the turtles he had seen not far from the shore came to the rescue. He seized them, turned them on their backs, cut their throats one at a time and drank their blood. His thirst slaked, he took the flesh from the shells, cleaned them, and then used them to collect and store rainwater. The largest ones held up to 55 litres (12 gallons) of water. He was rescued, with a very long beard, seven years later. He never wanted to see a turtle again.

✎ Emergency fire

If the matches run out and storms have doused the fire, do not despair. Before descending into barbaric savagery, you can light a fire using the heat of the sun and a carefully angled glass prism.

Anything that concentrates sunlight into a burning dot will do – spectacles, a magnifying glass, even the tiny camera lens in your mobile phone. Focus the sun's rays on to a nest of tinder. When it catches blow gently, then add the kindling. This is most effective at the hottest point of the day. Only a lunatic will try to make it work by moonlight.

Sod's Law decrees that at some point you will have to make fire without matches, at twilight, in the rain, or all three. It's getting dark, you need a fire and you're going to have to rely on primitive technology. Stop thinking negative thoughts about Cro-Magnon man – nasty, brutish and short: this stuff worked for thousands of years. It's why we have PlayStations, jet planes and iPods. Except they can't save your life. But a flint and steel can.

From the Iron Age right up to the invention of the friction match in 1827, flint and steel were the most common method of fire lighting. The combination still works. When you use a disposable lighter, your thumb rolls over the round metal bit, striking the flint and creating a spark, which ignites the gas.

A commercial firesteel can produce sparks of 3,000ºC (5,432ºF), which can easily light toilet paper or wood shavings. However, any sharp-edged rock and carbon-steel striker will suffice. You don't actually need flint. Any hard, nonporous rock with a glassy appearance – glass is too brittle – will do.

With a proper striker, you can get sparks off anything with a sharp edge – even petrified wood. The spark comes from shaving small pieces of steel off of the striker, with enough friction to heat them up to red hot. A striker has to be made of carbon steel. You can use the back of a knife or an 8cm (3-inch) piece of steel file. (Swiss Army knives have stainless-steel blades, so will not work).

Take the hard rock, with a sharp edge in one hand and the steel striker in the other. Place a piece of char cloth on top of the rock to catch the sparks. Char cloth or char paper is material that has been charred in the fire, then smothered in earth. Because it has been partially burned it is easily reignited by a spark. Any pure untreated cotton – handkerchiefs, denim jeans, canvas, cotton belts – will do, though thicker materials are better You have to burn the material thoroughly but not too much, or it dissolves into ash. Char cloth is the intermediate step between the striking and the tinder. It will catch a spark, and glow, but it will not ignite. Hold the striker loosely, and swing it straight down along the sharp edge of the rock as if you were trying to shave the striker with the rock. Take the glowing char cloth, and set it against your tinder, and blow on it gently until you get a flame.

When travelling, always store the char cloth in a waterproof container; if you have space, also keep some dry tinder as well. Stuck down your trousers it can make good insulation against the cold.

Bow drills, hand drills and fire ploughs

Yes, you can make fire by rubbing two sticks together, but there is a little more to it than that. For one thing, it needs a lot of practice. If you're intending to make fire with bow drills, hand drills and fire ploughs, make sure you really know how they work. Otherwise, you'll be eating raw food with blistered hands.

The principle behind all three devices is the same. Friction between hardwood and softwood produces enough heat to ignite wood shavings. These create an ember hot enough to start a tinder fire.

A bow drill, or *firebow*, is the most efficient but requires the most kit. The bow is a pliable but strong curved branch 50–75cm (20–30 inches) long. The string can be made from strips of animal hide or a bootlace. Then you need a hardwood spindle 1–2cm (0.5–0.8 inch) in diameter and 20–25cm (8–10 inches) long. The fireboard should be of a softer wood, roughly the same thickness as the spindle but wider and long enough to hold down with your foot. The final piece is the socket, which fits on top of the spindle and helps hold it down. This can be made from stone, bone or hardwood, and is crucial. If it fits the spindle snugly, it's much easier to get everything set up straight and running smooth.

Place the fireboard on flat ground. Make a hole for the spindle on the edge of the fireboard and the cut a notch to the centre of the hole. Place a piece of bark under the notch with your tinder nest close by and your left foot across the board to hold it steady 2.5cm (an inch) to the left of the hole.

Now wrap the bowstring once round the spindle and put that in the hole. Place the socket on top of the spindle and hold it securely, but not too hard, with your left hand. Your left hand and shin together have to keep the spindle vertical. Keeping the bow level, pull it back and forth with your right hand.

Smoke can come quickly, but don't stop! Keep bowing away until the notch is packed full of wood punk (tinder caused by the rotation). The punk near the spindle point should be black. You know you've achieved ember when the punk is smoking up a storm. Keep calm: the coal will continue to glow for a while. Blow on it gently or fan it with your hand. Place the glowing coal in the centre of your tinder nest, but don't wrap it so tight you smother it. Long steady breaths will help the flame come.

The hand drill requires longer and thinner spindles of a hollow softwood, while the fireboards are a thinner hardwood. This time the friction comes from your hands, rolling the spindle up and down between your palms. Do not let it roll out on to your fingers, as this loses speed and control. Bear down on the spindle as you twirl because downward pressure is equally important to spinning speed. Get it right and the tip of the spindle glows red, which, with a gentle blow, can ignite tinder. Because it's much harder than using a bow drill, blisters, bloody hands and rude words are common side effects.

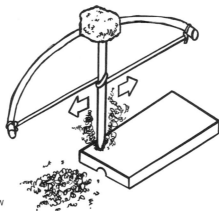

A working firebow

CASTAWAY

In the movie *Cast Away* (2000) Tom Hanks's character used a fire plough. It really is just rubbing two sticks together – or more specifically pushing one stick on to a base for a long, palm-blistering time. Take a softwood base a couple of centimetres thick and rub a hardwood plough stick back and forth to create a groove 15cm (6 inches) long. Continue faster and faster and the tinder you are making at the end of the groove will turn into a glowing ember.

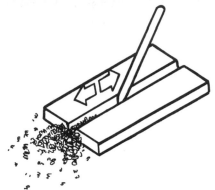

A working fire plough

If it's pissing down with rain and the ground is soaking wet, keeping the fire going will present continued challenges. Build your own little fireplace with one rock on either side with a large flat rock over the top. It should be shaped like a 'V' with a smaller hole at the back to carry away the smoke and a large opening at the front to provide adequate ventilation. The flat-rock roof protects the fire from the rain, and the rock side reflects the heat back at you, maximising the heat. The whole structure is a natural oven that keeps the coals hot all night, so it's easy to get going again in the morning. The flat roof is also an ideal cooking or warming surface. Who needs a kitchen range?

Wet logs don't burn very well, so wherever possible stack them near (but not too near) the fire to dry out. Once the campfire is blazing nicely, drag long logs across it. It will burn the middle and dry out the ends a treat.

DIRE STRAITS

EXTREME SHIT HAPPENS! Cannibalism

If all else fails, you can always eat one another. While there have been a few societies where cannibalism took on a religious and spiritual role, generally speaking eating your fellow man is taboo. It is the last resort, the time when the instinct to survive kicks in and overrides moral qualms.

When Uruguayan Air Force Flight 571 crashed into the Andes on 13 October 1972, sixteen survivors resorted to eating the bodies of the dead, many of whom were their friends and rugby teammates, during their 72 days in the mountains. While the movie *Alive* demonstrates the ingenuity the survivors displayed, for a true understanding of what drove them read Nando Parrado's *Miracle in the Andes*. He was one of the two men who trekked across the mountains for nine days to find rescue. At high altitude in freezing conditions where the body devours calories, they had no choice – which the world accepts.

The same was true of the Donner Party, a group of 87 California-bound settlers who were stranded in the Sierra Nevada mountains in 1847. With supplies running low, fifteen of the men, later known as the Forlorn Hope, set out on snowshoes for Sutter's Fort, about 160km (100 miles) away. Lost and out of food, four died when they were caught in a raging blizzard. Their bodies were eaten. Three more died and met the same fate. Then, after a month, virtually naked and close to death, seven snowshoers reached safety. Relief parties managed to rescue more than thirty of the stranded group – but not before some of them, too, had resorted to cannibalism.

While understanding that dire straits may require dire deeds, society as a whole perceives a moral difference between eating the bodies of the already dead and killing someone for their meat.

Alferd Packer was sentenced to forty years in prison for manslaughter, having killed and eaten five of his travelling companions while trapped in the Rocky Mountains. At his trial Packer claimed he went scouting for food and came back to discover Shannon Wilson Bell roasting human meat. As Bell rushed him, brandishing a hatchet, Packer shot and killed him. The judge was unimpressed, saying, 'Damn you, Alferd Packer! There were seven Dimmycrats in Hinsdale County and you ate five of them!' Until the day he died Packer claimed he was guilty of eating only dead bodies. Nobody chose to believe him, though recent forensic investigations of the bodies have proved he told the truth. He was a cannibal, not a murderer.

On 5 July 1884, the English yacht *Mignonette* sank off the Cape of Good Hope, stranding the crew of four on a 4-metre (13-foot) lifeboat. For twelve days they survived on two tins of turnips that the cabin boy Richard Parker had saved and whatever they could catch from the sea.

The captain, Tom Dudley, then proposed that Parker, who due to hunger and drinking seawater, was immobile and semiconscious, be sacrificed to feed the others. Edmund Brooks did not agree, but the next day, with no help in sight, Dudley said a prayer and with the blessing of the fourth survivor, Edwin Stephens, killed the boy. After four days they were rescued brought back to Falmouth and charged with murder.

The trial in Exeter makes for fascinating reading because the jury was sympathetic, understanding the very real perils of being lost at sea. It was also understood among the maritime community that if lives had to be sacrificed it was cabin boys who should be chosen on the somewhat spurious grounds that they generally had no family

or dependants. Eventually, after the case had been referred to a higher court in London, Brooks was acquitted. Dudley and Stephens were sentenced to death, though Queen Victoria later commuted their sentence to six months' imprisonment.

GET ME OUT OF HERE!

CASTAWAY

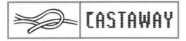 **CASTAWAY**

Things aren't going too well. Disease, thirst, starvation, natural disaster or internal community meltdown can all mean that remaining on the island is no longer an option. Perhaps you can't face another thigh cutlet from the mate you used to play football with.

You've got to get out.

If you are on a small island you have to head out to sea. Does it need saying that this is a seriously last resort? Apart from the risk of drowning through storms and waves, or smashing your craft on rock or reef, 'deep blue' is about as resource-scarce as you can get. Fresh food and water are extremely difficult to come by.

It's going to take planning. Is there any sort of usable craft already available? If you find a wrecked boat, bear in mind two things: first, that you are trusting your life to your expertise at boat repair; second, keeping out the water is not as easy as it may seem, particularly if there is no pitch or substitute to hand. If you are repairing a 'clinker' hull, where no caulking is needed because the planks overlap, you will need extremely sharp tools and precision cutting to get it right.

If there is nothing like this to find, you are going to have to make it. Forget about hollowing out huge tree stumps. Even using fire, this is a difficult procedure to get right, and it is even more difficult to keep from capsizing once it is on the water. Unless your family have been sailing the Pacific in dugout canoes for generations, you have to make a raft.

To prove that South American peoples could have populated Polynesia in pre-Columbus times, Norwegian explorer, writer, and all-round beardy, Thor Heyerdahl decided to conduct an experiment. In Peru, he put together the *Kon-Tiki*, a raft made with only indigenous materials and historical methods, as recorded in illustrations by Spanish conquistadors. He was determined to show that such an epic voyage was possible with only the most primitive technology.

The main hull of the raft was made of nine balsa-tree trunks about 14 metres (45 feet) long, lashed together with hemp ropes. Cross-pieces of balsa logs 5.5 metres (18 feet) long were tied across this hull at 90cm (3-foot) intervals to give lateral support. Pine splashboards clad the bow, and lengths of pine were used as centreboards.

The main mast was made of lengths of mangrove wood lashed together to form a A-frame about 9 metres (29 feet) high. Behind the mainmast was a cabin of plaited bamboo, roofed with banana leaf thatch. At the stern was a long steering oar of mangrove wood, with a blade of fir. No metal was used in the construction. The water for the trip was carried in bamboo tubes – 250 litres (440 pints) of it. For food they took 200 coconuts, sweet potatoes, bottle gourds and other assorted fruit and roots. Slightly spoiling the authenticity, the Quarter-Masters Department of the US Army provided field rations, tinned food and survival equipment.

The trip began on 28 April 1947. With five companions, Heyerdahl sailed it for 101 days over 6,920km (4,300 miles) across the Pacific Ocean. Along the way they boosted their diet with the plentiful numbers of fish they caught, particularly flying fish, 'dolphin' (a type of fish – not Flipper), yellowfin tuna and shark.

The raft worked, even if the theory, eventually, didn't. Now considered a classic of 'pseudo-archaeology', the theory has not survived modern DNA-checking methods. Nonetheless, the book of the adventure and the raft – museumed just outside Oslo – remain a classic of Borg-lookalike survival cool.

Making a raft

A basic raft can be even simpler than Thor's. Bamboo is ideal, although make sure you go for a two-layer model. Select thickish bamboo in about 3-metre (10-foot) lengths. Make a deck by fashioning holes at each end and the middle and passing through twine or some sort of homemade cable. Make a second deck to fit above the first and lash the two together.

Alternatively, collect logs and four medium-sized stakes with a bit of pliability about them. To find logs you may need to chop down a tree. To do so you first need to cut into it from both sides. First chop out a notch of 45 degrees. Before you have reached halfway, switch sides and chop another notch lower down. The tree will fall in the direction of the lower notch unless most of its branches are on one side, in which case it will fall in that direction no matter how many notches you cut into your tree trunk.

How to fell a tree

Once you have your logs, lay them on top of the stakes (see the diagram on page 199) and then place the other stakes on top. Tie each pair of stakes firmly together at either end — you may need a helper to stand on top of them to force them down — so that the logs are gripped between the staves. Notching the ends of these 'gripper bars' will stop the ropes or twine from slipping. Construct an A-frame to hold a rudder. This can be used to propel the raft if all else fails.

Make use of whatever is available. Oil drums are ideal, if they can be firmly attached to the main structure. It is even possible to make a raft by lashing together a number of dead seals — their blubber means that they float very well — although this is recommended only for short journeys. If nothing else, the appeal of being tied to the smell of decaying flesh might pall somewhat after a few days.

You will also need protection from the elements, hence Heyerdahl's bamboo and coconut cabin. As a minimum, you must have a windbreak and spray shield, or you could be cold beyond belief – and survival – long before you reach your destination. It's not a bad idea to have some sort of sea anchor as well. This can be improvised from any heavy object securely fastened to a line.

Rafts can also be used for lake or river transport or for fishing offshore. On a river, if there are rapids ahead, abandon ship without delay and head for the riverbank.

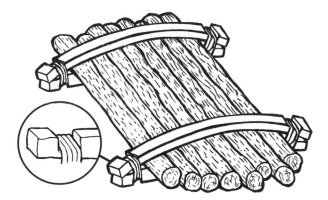

A basic raft

Get out of there

Test the raft thoroughly on safe water. Ensure you carry adequate water and food, and the means to collect water from the rain and to fish for food. Think very seriously about setting up and testing a solar still for water (see Page 182–3). Plan where everything is going to go. Space will be limited and some provisions – particularly anything spoiled by seawater – will need special storing.

If you are using several craft, work out who is the fittest to lead the fleet. The 'advance raft' should have the strongest people, but none of the vital equipment or supplies. As the 'vanguard' (particularly on rivers) they have

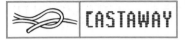 **CASTAWAY**

to be able to abandon their raft without losing vital supplies. Check out in advance any tides, currents and winds prevailing in the immediate area.

Think very hard about the challenges ahead. It's a new, watery environment that may be very different from what you have survived so far. Water will get everywhere, wrecking provisions, health and morale. Your eyes will suffer, so if your Oakleys haven't survived protect yourself from the glare of the sun off the water by making thin slits in a piece of tree bark and using natural string attached to each side to secure them to your face.

In a craft with no keel, it is possible to sail only downwind or at an angle of a maximum of 10 degrees away from the wind. If you have a keeled vessel, with a functioning rudder and boom, then much more is possible. Even miracles.

Bligh's epic voyage

After the mutiny on the *Bounty*, 33-year-old William Bligh and 18 other crew members loyal to him were set adrift in the ship's launch, an open boat, 7 metres (23 feet) long by 2 metres (6.56 feet) wide. They had a quadrant and a compass but no maps or charts; they also had canvas, lines, sails, 125 litres (28 gallons) of water, a small amount of dry pork, wine and rum and 68 kilos (150 pounds) of bread – rations for no more than five days. In most cases this would have been a death sentence.

Through sailing and rowing, the small party reached one of the nearby Friendly Islands. The snag was, they weren't that friendly. The Englishmen managed to collect a small quantity of water, breadfruit and coconuts before they were attacked by the island's inhabitants, who had seen that they were defenceless. One of their number was stoned to death and the others only narrowly made their escape.

Bligh now decided to head for the nearest European outpost, which he reckoned was the Dutch colony of Timor, an astonishing 6,440km (4,000 miles) away. The group were fortunate in one respect: Bligh had worked as Captain James Cook's navigator on his final voyage and was probably one of the most brilliant navigators who has ever lived. On the launch he had to use 'dead reckoning' – estimating his position using course, speed and time – to determine a course through Endeavour Passage, the Fijian islands and reefs and onwards.

Throughout most of the voyage, due to storms and high seas, there had to be two men bailing out water at all times. 'Among the hardships we were to undergo,' Bligh later wrote, 'that of being constantly wet was not the least: the nights were very cold, and at day-light our limbs were so benumbed, that we could scarce find the use of them.' The men were further weakened by their starvation rations. Bligh set shares at 28g (1 ounce) of bread and a 0.14 litre (0.25 pint) of water per man, three times a day a day (water was reasonably plentiful, since gallons could be collected during heavy rainstorms). They sometimes passed islands, but, remembering their earlier experience (and, no doubt, the grisly fate of Captain Cook ten years earlier), they dared not land, as they were more or less unarmed.

They did their best to catch a fish, and hooked one at last after ten days of dragging a line. But they lost the slippery bastard while trying to get it into the boat. It was a heartbreaking moment. Rations were reduced further on 25 May. 'At dawn of day,' Bligh reports, 'some of my people seemed half dead: our appearances were horrible; and I could look no way, but I caught the eye of some one in distress. Extreme hunger was now too evident.'

The next day, they had a stroke of luck. 'At noon some noddies came so near to us, that one of them was caught by hand. This bird is about the size of a small pigeon. I divided it, with its entrails, into 18 portions.' After this, seabirds became a vital lifeline. They were frequently caught by hand and then divided up, beak and all, with the blood delivered directly into the mouths of those most starving. On one occasion, two birds' stomachs were found to contain 'several flying-fish and small cuttlefish, all of which I saved to be divided for dinner'.

There was a growing sense of desperation, not helped by the discovery that someone had been stealing from the crew's scarce food supplies. And everyone was now ill. Bligh writes:

The general complaints of disease among us, were a dizziness in the head, great weakness of the joints, and violent tenesmus [painful inability to defecate or urinate], most of us having had no evacuation by stool since we left the ship. I had constantly a severe pain at my stomach.

So, when land was spotted on 29 May, it was worth risking landing to try to find supplies. Oysters and fresh water were collected before the boat set off again. Shortly afterwards they caught a small dolphin; they seem to have got better at fishing.

Thanks to Bligh's skill, arguably the single greatest feat of dead reckoning in the history of navigation, they arrived at Timor after a 41-day voyage. Apart from the man killed in the Friendly Islands, everyone had survived. But only just:

Our bodies were nothing but skin and bones, our limbs were full of sores, and we were clothed in rags; in this condition, with the tears of joy and gratitude flowing down our cheeks, the people of Timor beheld us with a mixture of horror, surprise, and pity.

Surviving at sea

Your most immediate threat is storms. In rough weather, keep everyone attached to the boat with lines, keep low on the raft and avoid sudden movements. Deploy the sea anchor from the bow. This will keep it facing into the wind and help prevent the craft from capsizing. If travelling in a fleet, tie the vessels together.

Man overboard!

First rule is, again, don't panic. The human body floats in seawater. People drown only because they become hypothermic or panic and inhale seawater. If it is not possible to regain your vessel, try to relax with your face down in the sea and arms stretched out in front of you. This may sound a bit Zen, but it helps conserve your energy. Lift your head up and tread water when you need to exhale. Take a deep breath and return to the relaxed position. Alternatively you can improvise a flotation bag by tying the legs of a pair of trousers. Then sweep them over your head to inflate and place the open end face down in the water to trap the air in the legs. Salvage any floating material that is to hand.

On board there must be routine and calm organisation. Keep watch 24 hours a day, checking for any damage to the vessel, and on the lookout for land, aircraft or ships, as well as seaweed, seabirds or shoals of fish. If a potential rescuer is spotted remember that any signal performed three times is understood internationally as a distress message. During daylight, use a mirror to signal for help. Point the mirror at the sun and flash the reflected spot on a nearby object. Then raise the mirror to your eye level and reach out as far as you can with your free hand, which should be open with the palm facing you, and making a 'V' between an extended thumb and fingers.

Catch the spot of light in the 'V' and turn your whole body and the mirror together, keeping the spot of light in the 'V' until the target aircraft or ship is also in the 'V'. The reflected sun will be bang on target; wobbling the mirror slightly will cause the brilliant reflected light to flash on and off. If a plane has spotted your signal it will tilt its wings or flash green signal lights.

Seabirds are seldom more than 160km (100 miles) away from land. They usually fly away from land in the morning and towards it in the late afternoon. Look out for driftwood, changes in the colour of the sea and cumulus clouds (see 'Cloud watching' in Chapter 4) nearby. In an otherwise clear sky they are likely to have formed over land.

If you are going to be away from land for any length of time, it is vital that you take every opportunity to conserve and replenish your supplies of food and water. Get that solar still up and running. Reduce water loss through sweating by cooling in any breeze there might be, dampening your clothes with seawater, or just having a dip over the side (check for dangerous fish and always have a line tied to the raft). Collect all the rainwater you can by rigging up canvas or sheets of plastic. And get fishing!

Fish and turtles will be attracted to the shade the raft provides. Net or spear them if you do not have lines. In the open sea what you might catch depends, of course, on where you are and when. In general, warm currents carry the most fish life. Let's assume you are in warm water (if you're on a raft across the North Sea, you'd probably be dead from exposure long before the fish course). In tropical and subtropical regions, there are a number of species that you could well find on the end of your line.

DORADO: These are also known as the mahi-mahi or dolphin, and are easy to catch because they will take any kind of bait or lure. They are easy to spear as they swim close to the raft or boat. They are excellent to eat cooked and are as good raw as any fish can be. Dorado meat also dries well. The only problem is that they thrash wildly when you take them out of the water, and can jump back in.

TRIGGER FISH: These will readily eat small chunks of anything. Try a wire leader on your smallest hook first. They can also be speared. To get a trigger fish to put down its trigger (the front spine on its dorsal fin), press on its forehead just in front of the spine and push the spine back. You will need a good knife, since its hide is extremely tough. If caught near a coral reef, the triggerfish could be poisonous from its diet. If in doubt, discard or soak the fillets in fresh water for a hour before eating.

TUNA: There are many types, ranging from 0.1 kg (0.22 pound) to over a ton. All have pointed noses and a bullet shape. You'd be lucky to get a tuna to take a baited hook but they will go for lures, which you need to retrieve very fast to ensure you get the fish. Do not try to dry leftover tuna, as it is far too oily and is susceptible to scromboid poisoning (this happens when the fish putrefies and releases histamine). Eat your fill and use the rest as bait.

WAHOO: Strong with very sharp teeth, wahoo bite lures readily; your only hope is catching a small one and on the end of your heaviest wire at the end of your heaviest line. They also jump and have been known to disembowel unwary anglers. Found near islands or ocean ridges in tropical seas, they are incredibly slimy fish, but among the best eating in the ocean. Don't worry about the ugly creature in its stomach. It's a parasite; they all have them.

SHARKS: You don't really want to do this, do you? Fishing for sharks from a homemade vessel is asking for trouble. If a shark takes bait intended for another fish just try to break the line as near the hook as possible. Give the line a sharp jerk. If you are determined or desperate enough and do catch one (for which you will need your heaviest wire and swivel), it may stay alive enough to bite you and go on biting for a long time. It might also chew through your raft.

Try to kill it before bringing it on board. The simplest method is to jab an oar into its mouth to keep it occupied, and then stab it in the eye with your longest knife. Drag it in tail first and cut off the head while it's still hanging

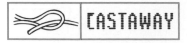
in the water so any random thrashes don't have those teeth on the end of them. Sharks must be cleaned as soon as possible, as they pee through their skin and the taste can infect the whole body. Don't eat the liver. If there seem to be few sharks around, and you see this is a bad thing, here's a trick that the fishermen of Samoa use. Taking advantage of the shark's excellent hearing, they make a shark attractor of coconut shells halved and strung together on a stick. This is submerged in the water and shaken vigorously to lure curious sharks, which are then speared.

SEAWEED: This can be found floating in clumps far out to sea. Do not eat it if water is short, but it is worth hauling aboard anyway as it often provides a home for small fish, shrimps and small crabs. And, if raw seabird meat is your thing (or if you are desperate enough), make a grab at the seabirds that come visiting. Alternatively, use a floating lure attached to a large hook. When the seabird comes to investigate, give the line a sharp tug and hope that you hook the bird. Enjoy!

Escape overland

Before you go ...
Whether you are leaving by sea or by land, it is essential that you leave details of where you have gone, and when. If you are travelling overland, leave markers showing your route. It may take an hour or two, but make sure that your fire is safely extinguished.

As with taking to the high seas, attempting a long hike to freedom needs careful preparation and risk assessment. Bear in mind that you are unlikely to travel much more than 3km (about 2 miles) an hour. If you have sick or injured people among the group, they should stay behind while a selection of the strongest go for help.

You will need food and water and some sort of pack for carrying it, and, of course footwear is all important. Take the makings of a simple shelter with you, and some tinder. Study the weather to find the best time to set out.

You should have some idea of the surrounding terrain. Investigate the first part of your route as much as you can, have a clear idea on the direction and then try to keep to it, if necessary by checking that your tracks head in a straight line. If you have no idea where the nearest human settlement might be, your best bet is to find a watercourse and head downstream. The river can also provide food and water, or even allow you to travel by raft.

If travelling in a group, don't just stroll along in a jumbled crowd as if you were walking off a good Sunday lunch. Instead, you should plan a formation, with a scout at the front, finding the best route, and a number two behind him or her, checking that the correct overall direction is maintained. In larger groups, everyone should have a responsibility for one other person. This, along with frequent head counts, prevents stragglers being lost.

It's not a race

You will probably be carrying much more than you usually would if you were walking to work, or just taking a brisk stroll through the woods or park. Bear this in mind when setting your pace. Tired hikers are far more likely to twist an ankle or sustain some other sort of injury. Be guided by your heartbeat. Find a speed at which you are not exerting yourself on flat ground . When going uphill, reduce this pace so that you maintain an even heartbeat, even if it seems painfully slow. In the long run, those who keep a steady pace burn fewer calories and can travel further, albeit more slowly. Mixed groups must set the pace to the slowest members. Stop every hour to rest – this gives you a good chance to communicate with each other if you are in a group, check your directions and deal with minor ailments such as blisters. Don't stop for too long, though: this can lead to a drop in your body temperature and stiffening of the muscles. Keep going. Just around the next corner...

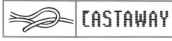
SHIT HAPPENS! Serious medical disasters

He's not breathing

Four to six minutes after the heartbeat and breathing stop, brain damage sets in so start CPR (cardiopulmonary resuscitation) immediately. Here's a summary of the CPR steps:

1. Lay the victim down, face up.
2. Check that the airway is clear. To open it, pull the chin forward by holding the sides of the victim's lower jaw and lifting with both hands.
3. If he/she is not breathing, hold the victim's nose and exhale two full breaths deeply into the mouth. The chest should rise and fall. If it does not, tilt the victim's head back a little by pushing back on the forehead and check to see if anything is blocking the throat.
4. Check the pulse at the carotid artery in the groove in the neck created by the trachea and the large strap muscles of the neck. It will take five or ten seconds to find a pulse. If there is a pulse, continue rescue breathing at a rate of twelve breaths a minute, or one every five seconds. If there is no pulse, start compressing the heart. Depress the lower part of the sternum (breast bone) about 5cm (2 inches). Push down 80–100 times a minute.
5. Check the carotid pulse again after one minute and then every five minutes. If you feel a pulse, stop the compression.
6. Check the eyes from time to time. If the pupils contract when exposed to light, the brain is getting blood and oxygen.
7. If you are giving CPR by yourself, administer fifteen compressions at a rate of 80–100 a minute, then give two breaths. If you have help, at the end of the two breaths, verify the lack of pulse and breathing for 5 seconds. Then give two deep breaths and continue on the 15:2 cycle.

Fractures

Immobilise fractures. If you have nothing you can use for a splint, strap the broken part to the opposite side. Duct tape works well for strapping broken bones, but wrap cloth or paper underneath the tape so that it doesn't stick to the skin, and don't make it tight enough to hinder circulation.

The most common fracture is that of the wrist. If you are brave enough, there is a painful and chancy way to reset it. Tie the fingers of the damaged hand to a tree and lean back with your body weight until you feel the broken bones jump back into position. Then bind on splints. Like any fracture, it will be painful for a couple of days, but after three weeks – if the process has worked – it should be fine.

Hypothermia

As blood is taken from the brain to warm the key organs in the torso, you start to get irrational. The biggest danger is that it takes away your will to help yourself. You are dying and you don't give a damn.

Cold lowers your ability to think, and your ability to think about anything but getting warm again. It sneaks up on you before you really notice. Before you know it you are finding it hard to move – you want to sleep, you want to forget about your goal until tomorrow. The trouble is, your goal is survival *today*; tomorrow may be too late.

Once someone has become hypothermic, wrapping up will not help them – they need external heat, from fire, hot drinks or another body. Do not rub or massage the victim's extremities, as this takes blood away from their core and vital organs. Put the victim in a sleeping bag with another person whose body temperature is still normal. Share body heat, concentrating on the head and torso. Both bodies need to be stripped for adequate heat transfer to take place, and it is worth noting that, for some strange reason of chemistry, this heat transfer is 5 per cent more effective if the people are of opposite sex. But don't get carried away: as the hypothermic victim warms up he/she is at risk of cardiac arrest. If the heart stops, immediately hit the victim hard in the middle of the chest. If that does not work, perform CPR.

Bleeding
Serious bleeding can kill very quickly. Stop it by applying pressure to the wound with a piece of folded cloth. A shirt works fine. Press hard and keep pressing until the bleeding stops. If the blood is squirting or comes out in pulses, you may have to stick a finger in the wound to press down on the artery. Do not attempt to stitch the wound.

Shock
Shock can occur as a result of a broken bone, loss of blood, inadequate blood circulation or lack of oxygen, among other causes. The skin of a person in shock is usually pale, cool and damp. Their breathing is rapid and shallow, and their pulse is weak but fast, over 100 beats a minute. The victim may also feel faint and nauseous. Do the following;

- Have victim lie down with their feet higher than their head.
- Keep them warm, but not so much that they are sweating.
- If there is no wound to head or stomach, give them water with one teaspoon of salt per litre (half a pint). Do not give liquids to anyone with an abdominal or head injury.
- Never give a shock victim alcohol in any form.

Burns
For minor or moderate burns apply cold fresh water. Do not use saltwater. If the burned area is dirty, wash it gently with water and

soap, if you have it. For more serious burns do not remove bits of flesh stuck to the wounds. Apply, if possible, 1-per-cent sulphadiazine silver cream and cover the area with a sterile dressing. Change the dressing daily, or more often if it soaks up a lot of fluid or starts to smell. Do not pull the dressing off; instead, soak it off with fresh water.

POSTSCRIPT

(SURVIVING) THE REAL WORLD

CASTAWAY

'Leaving Tuin at the end of the year, and readjusting to "normal" life was the hardest thing I've had to do. The truth is, I don't think I ever have "adjusted".'

Lucy Irvine, *Castaway*

Robinson Crusoe came to love his new life on his island better than his old. He learned to count his blessings, and to understand what is important. 'I began sensibly to feel how much more happy this life I now led was, with all its miserable circumstances,' he says, 'than the wicked, cursed, abominable life I led all the past part of my days.'

Being a castaway will radically alter your view of the world. Behaviour reflected back by people you trust will help you learn about yourself. You can then decide to change or not. This means clearing away a lot of the debris with which society has encumbered us, enabling us to become more honest and open, in other words to become childlike in our outlook. For a long time groups have been used to help treat mental illness, alcoholism and other addictions. Living in a group surviving *in extremis* teaches us about ourselves and about each other and that both are essential to our survival as a species.

For most people in the West, castaway life offers an escape from the mountain of trivia, unnecessary information and wasteful stuff that clutters our lives (and destroys the planet). Maybe one day we will all have learned to live in a sustainable way.

Alternatively, you may have found that spending all day catching, preparing and cooking a meal that takes you ten minutes to eat is not progress at all. Perhaps being hungry, cold, tired and ill is not such a rewarding experience. Most of those who have lived through extreme survival experiences testify that in many ways it enriched their lives. But that depends on you: some are strengthened by their ordeals, some crushed by them.

If nothing else, you will be given a new insight into the true necessities of life. Plus a fund of great stories.

Failing that, there's always poetry.

Castaway Kipling

If you can make a bed when all about you
Are sleeping on the ground and getting sore
If you can trust yourself when doubts surround you
But still do it, and come back for more
If you can lead a group with care but also follow,
Eat a beetle larva, chew and swallow
If you can feed yourself and not shrink in size
And use the latrine (don't deal in flies!)
If you can fish and catch and trap
Dine like a king or live on scraps
If you can build from nothing a home
And conquer loneliness, all alone
If you no longer need car or train
But can live off the earth, the sun and rain
If you can sail through storms and squalls
But deal with everything that befalls
Yours is the Earth and everything that's in it,
And − which is more − you'll be a Man, my son!

Index

Italics indicate boxed text.